While every precaution has been taken in the [ ]
book, the publisher assumes no responsibility for errors or omissions,
or for damages resulting from the use of the information contained
herein.

STOCK PRICE ANALYSIS THROUGH STATISTICAL AND
DATA SCIENCE TOOLS: AN OVERVIEW

First edition. April 30, 2021.

Copyright © 2021 Vinaitheerthan Renganathan.

ISBN: 978-1393996347

Written by Vinaitheerthan Renganathan.

Stock price analysis through Statistical and Data Science tools: An Overview
Vinaitheerthan Renganathan

Title: Stock price analysis through Statistical and Data Science tools: An Overview

Author: Vinaitheerthan Renganathan

Edition: 1st Edition

Copyright: © 2021 Vinaitheerthan Renganathan

Stock price analysis through Statistical and Data Science tools: An Overview

Preface

Stock price analysis involves different methods such as fundamental analysis and technical analysis which is based on data related to price movement of the stock in the past. Price of the stock is affected by various factors such as company's performance, current status of economy and political factor. These factors play an important role in supply and demand of the stock which makes the price to be volatile in the short term. Investors and stock traders aim to book profit through buying and selling the stocks. There are different statistical and data science tools are being used to predict the stock price.

Data Science and Statistical tools assume only the stock price's historical data in predicting the future stock price. Statistical tools include measures such as Graph and Charts which depicts the general trend and time series tools such as Auto Regressive Integrated Moving Averages (ARIMA) and regression analysis.

Data Science tools include models like Decision Tree, Support Vector Machine (SVM), Artificial Neural Network (ANN) and Long Term and Short Term Memory (LSTM) Models.

Current methods include carrying out sentiment analysis of tweets, comments and other social media discussion to extract the hidden sentiment expressed by the users which indicate the positive or negative sentiment towards the stock price and the company.

The book provides an overview of the analyzing and predicting stock price movements using statistical and data science tools using R open source software with hypothetical stock data sets. It provides a short introduction to R software to enable the user to understand analysis part in the later part.

The book will not go into details of suggesting when to purchase a stock or what at price. The tools presented in the book can be used as a guiding tool in decision making while buying or selling the stock.

Vinaitheerthan Renganathan

Chapter 1: Introduction

L et us start with introduction of stock market, its products and theories, financial ratios involved with respect to the stocks.

Stock Market

Stock market or Stock exchange facilitates the trading of shares owned by publically listed companies. It is mostly regulated by the government or individual governing body. Stock is a type of security which provides proportionate ownership of the company to the holder of the stock. The term share and stock refers mostly the same but share can be interpreted as a micro level indictor of the ownership in the company. Stock is used as a generic term while share is used to denote a particular company.

Most of the financial stock market uses term called index which comprised of groups of stocks which are included based on certain criteria such as market capitalization and the same criteria is used as weights to calculate the index. S&P 500 index is started with 3 stocks and now it uses 500 stocks to calculate the index. If the prices of stocks which are included in the index rose then the stock market index will also raise.

Stock market consists of different products such individual stocks, mutual funds, bonds, debts, derivatives and commodities.

Mutual funds are held by organization which pools money from individual investors and invest in stocks and other products in the financial stock market such bonds and debts.

Bonds in the stock market represent a loan instrument which helps the organizations and government to raise funds for their capital investment. It provides a fixed income to the owner of the bond and has a maturity date.

Derivatives include forward, future and options contracts. Forward contract is an agreement between parties or players in the stock market to buy or sell an asset or stock at predetermined price. Future contract is similar to forward contract and options contract is flexible and one has the right but not the obligation to buy or sell the asset or stock at a predetermined price. If options holder does not exercise his contract then the contract can be discontinued by paying a nominal fee involved in the option which saves the investor from the downside.

Stock price prediction is carried out using technical and fundamental analysis. There are different players involved in the stock market such as individual traders, investors, mutual fund managers, stock brokers and stock exchange regulators. Stock price is affected by the supply and demand of the traded stock which is affected by various factors such as

- Company's performance
  - Own performance
  - Compared to competitor
- Number of share holders
- Number of shares publicly traded
- Particular industries future growth prospect
- Economic indicators
  - Gross Domestic Product
  - Inflation
  - Financial Institution's rate of interest
- Government policy decisions
- Political environment
- News and rumors about the stock

Stock price reflects all the above factors which are already happened and future price will be affected as and when the new information received by the participants and it is known as Efficient Market Hypothesis.

Dow Theory

Dow Theory emphasizes on the following

- All the news and financial results are already discounted in the stock price
- Every market includes three basic trends. Primary, Secondary and Minor trend where primary trend provides long term trend and lasts for years such as bull (increasing trend phase) or bear phase(decreasing trend phase). Secondary trend is a one which lasts for weeks to months and indicates a pullback or reversal. Minor trend indicates short term fluctuations

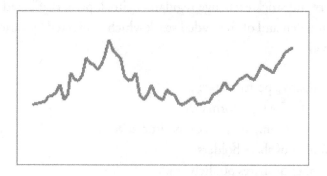

- All the components of the stock market should confirm with each other

Elliot Theory

Elliot Theory suggests that the bull or bear phase will contain patterns represented by waves. The waves might repeat a specified number of times during the bull or bear phase.

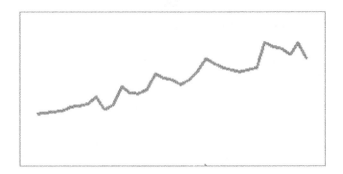

Head and Shoulder Theory

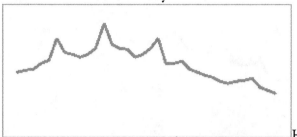

Head and shoulder theory says if a peak is followed by a high peak and then a similar peak, it represents a head and two shoulder pattern. If the stock price drops below the second shoulder bottom then there is a trend reversal in a bull market. Similarly the inverted shoulder indicates a reversal in bear market.

Behavioral Finance Theory

As per the Behavioral finance theory the stock prices are affected by the greed and fear of the participants. Greed will push price and Fear will bring down the price of the stock.

Financial Ratios related to stocks

There are important financial ratios are available which indicates the current status of the stock and the company.

a. Earnings per Share (EPS) Ratio

It indicates the Earning per share which is arrived from dividing the company's net income divided by the total number of shares held by the shareholders during the year. EPS will be more if income is increased while number of shares decreased during that particular year.

a. Price-Earning (P/E) Ratio

It indicates the ratio of share price to the Earning Per Share. A high P/E ratio means the investors willing to pay more for the stock or sometimes the share price might be overvalued. Similarly a low P/E might indicate a downward trend.

a. Debit – Equity Ratio

Debit Equity ratio indicates the ratio of outstanding debt to shareholders total share value. A low Debit Equity ratio means the companies performing well.

a. Operating Profit Margin

Operating profit margin is arrived by dividing the operating profit (profit before tax) by total revenue. If it is higher, then the company is performing well.

Technical Analysis of stock price includes Statistical and Data Science tools which are given below:

a. Graphs and plots
b. Time series models
    i. Simple Moving Average
    ii. Exponential Moving Average

a. Machine Learning Models
    i. Decision tree
    ii. Naïve Bayes
    iii. Support Vector Machine (SVM)
    iv. Artificial Neural Network (ANN)
b. Deep Learning Models
    i. Long Short Term Memory Models (LSTM)

Apart from the numeric data analysis, currently unstructured data is also used for analyzing the stock price. User's opinion, comments and reviews found in the social media sites, trading sites provides wealth of information in the form of text. Text mining, Natural Language processing and Sentiment analysis helps us to extract the hidden sentiment expressed by the users which indicate the positive or negative sentiment towards the stock price and the company.

Currently High Frequency Trading (HFT) systems which uses automated system to place multiple orders in a fraction of time and uses algorithm to take decisions either to buy or sell the stocks. The automated systems takes decisions based on the available information and decisions are taken in a fraction of seconds. HFT systems are used by the institutional investors and mostly it does not include human intervention in decision making.

The following sections of the book mainly focus on technical analysis of the stock price prediction.

Reference

1. Edwards, R. D., Magee, J., & Bassetti, W. C. (2018). Technical

analysis of stock trends. CRC press.

2. Nazário, R. T. F., e Silva, J. L., Sobreiro, V. A., & Kimura, H. (2017). A literature review of technical analysis on stock markets. The Quarterly Review of Economics and Finance, 66, 115-126.

3. Deng, S., Mitsubuchi, T., Shioda, K., Shimada, T., & Sakurai, A. (2011, December). Combining technical analysis with sentiment analysis for stock price prediction. In 2011 IEEE ninth international conference on dependable, autonomic and secure computing (pp. 800-807). IEEE.

4. Ariyo, A. A., Adewumi, A. O., & Ayo, C. K. (2014, March). Stock price prediction using the ARIMA model. In 2014 UKSim-AMSS 16th International Conference on Computer Modelling and Simulation (pp. 106-112). IEEE.

5. Emioma, C. C., & Edeki, S. O. (2021, January). Stock price prediction using machine learning on least-squares linear regression basis. In Journal of Physics: Conference Series (Vol. 1734, No. 1, p. 012058). IOP Publishing.

6. Emioma, C. C., & Edeki, S. O. (2021, January). Stock price prediction using machine learning on least-squares linear regression basis. In Journal of Physics: Conference Series (Vol. 1734, No. 1, p. 012058). IOP Publishing.

7. Lin, Y., Guo, H., & Hu, J. (2013, August). An SVM-based approach for stock market trend prediction. In The 2013 international joint conference on neural networks (IJCNN) (pp. 1-7). IEEE.

8. Vui, C. S., Soon, G. K., On, C. K., Alfred, R., & Anthony, P. (2013, November). A review of stock market prediction with Artificial neural network (ANN). In 2013 IEEE international conference on control system, computing and engineering (pp. 477-482). IEEE.

9. Singh, R., & Srivastava, S. (2017). Stock prediction using deep

learning. Multimedia Tools and Applications, 76(18), 18569-18584.

10. Bharathi, S., & Geetha, A. (2017). Sentiment analysis for effective stock market prediction. International Journal of Intelligent Engineering and Systems, 10(3), 146-154.

11. Pramudya, R., & Ichsani, S. (2020). Efficiency of technical analysis for the stock trading. International Journal of Finance & Banking Studies, 9(1), 58-67.

12. Schannep, J. (2008). Dow theory for the 21st century. Technical Indicators for Improving Your Investment Results, 4.

13. Poser, S. W. (2003). Applying Elliot Wave Theory Profitably (Vol. 169). John Wiley & Sons.

14. Tabar, S., Sharma, S., & Volkman, D. (2021). Stock Market Prediction Using Elliot Wave Theory and Classification. International Journal of Business Analytics (IJBAN), 8(1), 1-20.

15. Savin, G., Weller, P., & Zvingelis, J. (2007). The predictive power of "head-and-shoulders" price patterns in the US stock market. Journal of Financial Econometrics, 5(2), 243-265.

Chapter 2: R Software

We will be using R open source software and its Integrated Development environment R studio to carry out the staock price analysis including graphical analysis and stock price prediction.

R software and its IDE R Studio can be downloaded from the below websites:

1. https://cran.r-project.org/bin/windows/base/
2. https://rstudio.com/products/rstudio/download/

R software has rich packages developed by R community which helps the users to use it for their requirement and also packages can be created from the existing packages. R has a default stat package which has functions related to basic statistical measures and data handling.

We will be using R studio to execute the R code. R studio contains four windows – Code, Environment, output, help windows.

The packages need to be installed using install.packages statement and called into the R studio environment using library statement.

Different data sources such Excel files, CSV files and text files can be used in the R studio environment. To use an Excel file we need install xlsx package and call it through library statement as follows

```
Install.packages('xlsx)
Library(xlsx)
```

WE NEED TO DEFINE A working directory using setwd statement as follows:

```
Setwd('c:/test')
```

R uses objects to handle data such vectors, strings, numbers and assignment operator is used to assign values to the objects

```
Stockprice<-c(100,105,99,88)
print(Stockprice)
```

HERE C IS THE FUNCTION which assigns values the numeric vector Stockprice. Print statement print the values of the variable or numeric vector as below in the R studio console

```
[1] 100 105  99  88
```

Data frame

Data frame is normally used in R to store the data which is used for further processing. Data frame is a table or matrix kind of object which holds value of the data set in column and row form. Each column represents the variable and each row or record contains the value for that particular variable

We can define the stock price information as data frame as below.

```
trdate<-as.Date(c("2021-01-01","2021-01-02","2021-
01-03","2021-01-04","2021-01-05"))
open<-c(95,100,105,117,98)
close<-c(98,107,113,115,108)
stockdata<-data.frame(trdate,open,close)
print(stockdata)
```

The above data frame consists of 3 variables and 5 rows or records. The obtained data frame is given below

```
  trdate open close
1 2021-01-01  95   98
2 2021-01-02 100  107
3 2021-01-03 105  113
4 2021-01-04 117  115
5 2021-01-05  98  108
```

We can retrieve the particular column or record by specifying corresponding index value.

```
stockdata[1,3]
stockdata[2,]
```

THE FOLLOWING VALUES are obtained

```
stockdata[1,3]
[1] 98
stockdata[2,]
      trdate open close
2 2021-01-02  100   107
```

We will import sample stock price xlsx file obtained from Bombay Stock Exchange, India (BSE India) through read.xlsx statement which is having the following fields:

1. Date
2. Open Price
3. High Price
4. Low Price
5. Close price
6. Number of shares

The imported data will be assigned to data frame. The contents of the data frame can be displayed using head statement. It displays the first 5 rows of the excel file along with column names.

```
data1<-Read.xlsx('test.xlsx')
head(data1)
```

```
Date   Open.Price  High.Price  Low.Price
Close.Price    No.of.Shares
1 2020-01-01    334.50   335.85   332.25
334.0816    616224
2 2020-01-02    334.85   339.85   333.40
336.9444    882070
3 2020-01-03    338.00   338.00   332.10
335.0434    761014
4 2020-01-06    332.00   332.00   317.90
322.0016    1422311
5 2020-01-07    324.00   327.00   315.55
320.2707    1798194
6 2020-01-08    312.70   321.40   311.00
```

WE CAN ALSO USE R PACKAGES such as quantmod, tidyquant, BatchGetSymbols and stocks can be used to get the stock price related data. The following code uses quantmod package to get the Google stock price from 01-01-2020 till 31-03-2021 from the US stock market.

```
Library(quantmod)
D<-getSymbols("GOOG", from = '2020-01-01',
      to = "2021-03-01",warnings = FALSE,
      auto.assign = TRUE)
```

```
head(GOOG)
```

The following code gives the first five rows of downloaded stock price data

```
        GOOG.Open   GOOG.High   GOOG.Low
        GOOG.Close              GOOG.Volume
        GOOG.Adjusted
2020-01-02   1341.55   1368.14 1341.550
1367.37    1406600    1367.37
2020-01-03   1347.86   1372.50 1345.544
1360.66    1186400    1360.66
2020-01-06   1350.00   1396.50 1350.000
1394.21    1732300    1394.21
2020-01-07   1397.94   1402.99 1390.380
1393.34    1502700    1393.34
2020-01-08   1392.08   1411.58 1390.840
1404.32    1528000    1404.32
2020-01-09   1420.57   1427.33 1410.270
1419.83    1500900    1419.83
```

References

1. R Core Team (2020). R: A language and environment for statistical computing. R Foundation for Statistical Computing, Vienna, Austria. URL https://www.R-project.org/.
2. RStudio Team (2020). RStudio: Integrated Development for R. RStudio, PBC, Boston, MA URL http://www.rstudio.com/.
3. https://www.bseindia.com/
4. https://cran.r-project.org/package=xlsx
5. https://cran.r-project.org/package=quantmod
6. https://cran.r-project.org/package=tidyquant
7. https://cran.r-project.org/package=BatchGetSymbols
8. https://cran.r-project.org/package=stocks

Chapter 3: Graphical Analysis

Different graphical analysis tools are used to predict and know the trend of the stock price. Box plot, Line graph, Candlestick and Relative Strength Index chart

Box Plot

Box plot provides the information about the distribution of stock price in terms of median, first quartile and 3rd quartile values.

- Median value - 50% of the stock prices are below that value when the stock prices are ordered from high to low price
- First Quartile value – 25% of the stock prices are below that value when the stock prices are ordered from high to low price
- Third Quartile – 75% of the stock prices are below that value when the stock prices are ordered from high to low price
- It includes maximum and minimum value of the series
- It also indicates any outlier values if any in the stock price.

We will plot the Box plot using R software ggplot2 package. We will be installing and defining the same in the R studio environment. We will be installing lubridate and dpylr package to handle date variable and data related function in the sample stock dataset.

```
library(ggplot2)
library(lubridate)
library(dpylr)
```

THE FOLLOWING GGPLOT statement provides overall box plot with following

Median – Central line,

First Quartile – Bottom of the box

Third Quartile Value - Top line on the box

Line starting point and ending point denotes minimum and maximum values

```
ggplot(data=data1) +
  geom_boxplot( aes(y=Close.Price),fill='#32a2a8',
color="black") +
  labs(y="Closing Price",x="Overall")
```

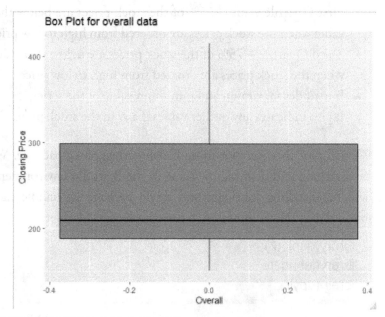

THE ABOVE VALUES CAN be obtained using summary function

```
summary(data1$Close.Price)
```

```
 Min.  1st Qu. Median   Mean 3rd Qu.  Max.
150.8  188.6  208.8   243.5  298.1   415.0
```

WE CAN ALSO GET THE month wise box plot to see the monthly variation. To do that we need to extract year and date values and store it in a variable in a new data frame using the following code

```
dm<-month(data1$Date)
dmname<-month(data1$Date,label=TRUE)
year<-year(data1$Date)
data2<-data.frame(year,dm,clg,dmname)
```

HERE WE HAVE USED MONTH function of the lubridate twice one for numeric value of the month and another for string value of the month.

We need to create the following

a. A new variable which include month in numeric, month in string
b. Set the new variable as factor
c. Reorder the factor variable with integer value and select the substr month & year to be used as x axis label for the plot

```
d <- paste(data2$dm,"\n",
data2$dmname,"\n",data2$year)
d<-factor(d)
d<-reorder(substr(d,3,15), sort(as.numeric(d)))
```

THE FOLLOWING GGPLOT2 statement provides the month wise box plot

```
ggplot(data=data2)  +
  geom_boxplot( aes(x=d , y=clg, fill=factor(year))) +
  labs(x="Month"  ,y="Closing Price", fill="Year")
```

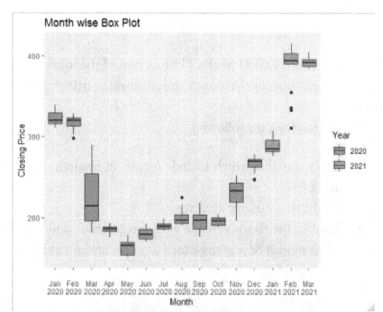

HERE FROM THE ABOVE box we can see that there is change between year 2020 and 2021 values and the overall trend is also positive. It also includes some outliers among the monthly box plots.

Line graph

Line graph helps us to know the trend in the stock price which indicates the direction of the trend even when there is fluctuation seen during different sub periods.

The following ggplot2 statement will provide us the line graph. Here we will use the original data set data1 for plotting line graph. Here we will use geom_line() and geom_point() option.

```
ggplot(data=data1, aes(x=Date , y=clg)) +
  geom_line() +
  labs(x="Month" ,y="Closing Price")+
  geom_point(colour="blue")
```

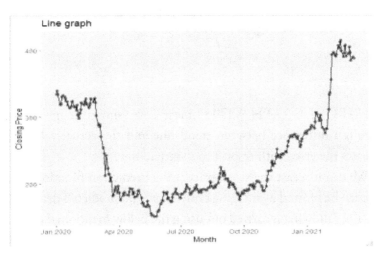

WE CAN ALSO USE ADD linear trend and quadratic trend lines to the line graph using smooth function option of ggplot. Here we will use the linear model with formula y ~ x

```
ggplot(data=data1, aes(x=Date, y=clg)) +
  labs(x="Month" ,y="Closing Price")+
  geom_point(colour="red")+
  geom_smooth(method = "lm",formula = y ~ x)
```

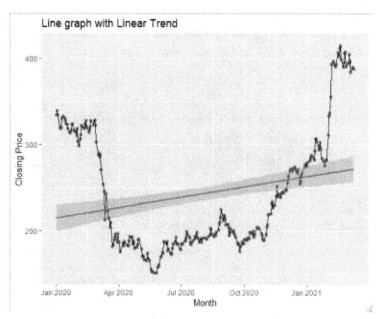

Line graph with Linear Trend

THE ABOVE GRAPH WITH Linear Trend shows an upward trend. There is a difference between trend line and the actual value which indicates the error with respect to the trend line.

We can forecast the stock price using prediction function and the same can be plotted by merging both actual and predicted data sets into one. The following is carried out using the below mentioned code

a. New dataset with date values for next 15 days created(newdata2)

b. Lm model is created with old data set

c. Prediction function is used to predict Closing price for the next 15 days

d. New type variable is created in both new and old data set

e. Only three variables selected from old data set and named it as m1

f. Both m1 and new data set is merged to give total which will be used for plotting the values

```
newdata2<-read.xlsx('newdata.xlsx',sheetIndex =
1)
model <- lm(Close.Price ~ Date, data=data1)
newdata1$Close.Price<-predict
(model,newdata1)
newdata1$type<-c("Pred")
data1$type<-c("Actual")
m1<-data1[c("Date","Close.Price", "type")]
```

The following ggplot code provides us linear trend along with actual and predicted values. Here we have used the following

1. Geom_line function along with type variable to show both the actual and predicted values line.
2. Geom_smooth function to show the trend line
3. Fill option in the ggplot function provides all the three lines.

```
ggplot(data=total, aes(x=Date, y=Close.Price,
Fill=type)) +
    labs(x="Month" ,y="Closing Price")+
    geom_line(aes(color = type, linetype =
type,size=0.1)) +
    geom_smooth(method = "lm",formula = y ~ x
)+
    labs(title="Line graph with Linear Trend and
Prediciton")
```

Here red color line is actual data, blue color line is trend line and blue line with blue shade denotes predicted values.

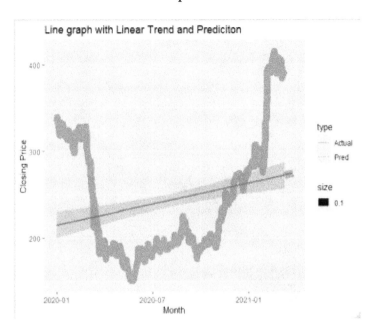

THE FOLLOWING CODE gives quadratic trend line using the geom_smooth function with formula y ~ x+x^2

```
ggplot(data=data1, aes(x=Date,y=clg)) +
  labs(x="Month" ,y="Closing Price")+
  geom_point(colour="blue")+
  geom_smooth(method = "lm",formula = y ~ x +
```

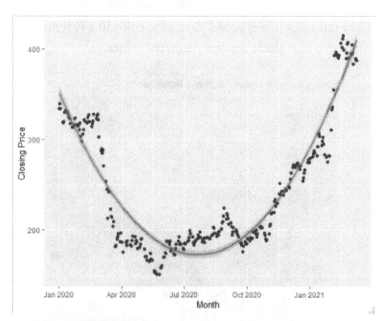

HERE THE QUADRATIC trend line is closer to the actual values than the linear trend.

As in the previous linear trend we can predict the next 15 days closing price using the following code. Here we will be using quadratic function in the lm function and we need to convert date into numeric values before using it the quadratic function.

```
Library(quantmod)
  model1 <- lm(Close.Price ~
as.numeric(Date)+I((as.numeric(Date))^2),
data=data1)
  newdata2$x2<-
predict(model1,newdata=newdata2)
  newdata2$type<-c("Pred")
  names(newdata2)[names(newdata2) == "x2"] <-
"Close.Price"
  total2 <- rbind(m1, newdata2)
  ggplot(data=total2, aes(x=Date,
y=Close.Price,Fill=type)) +
  labs(x="Month" ,y="Closing Price")+
  geom_line(aes(color = type, linetype = type,size =
0.5)) +  geom_smooth(method = "lm",formula = y ~
x + I(x^2))+labs(title="Line  graph with Quadratic
Trend and Prediction")
```

HERE RED COLOR LINE is actual data, blue color line is trend line and blue line with blue shade denotes predicted values.

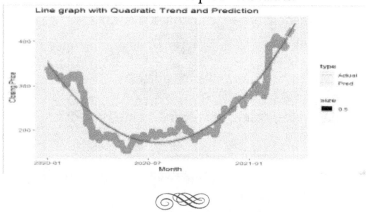

CANDLE STICK CHART

Candle Stick chart is similar to box plot but it is defined by high, low, open and close values of stock price. It is mostly used at daily stock trading level. Each day stock trading will be represented by one candle where it include high, close, open and low price in an upward movement and will contain high, open, close and low price in an downward movement. Upward candle stick and downward candle stick are represented by green and red colour respectively.

Plotly package help us to produce Candlestick chart. The following code gives the basic candle stock chart.

```
Library(plotly)
cdata <- data.frame(Date=data1,coredata(data1))
cdata <- tail(df, 360)
P1 <- cdata %>% plot_ly(x = ~Date,
type="candlestick",
          open = ~Date.Open.Price, close =
~Date.Close.Price,
          high = ~Date.High.Price, low =
~Date.Low.Price)
p1 <- p1 %>% layout(title = "Candlestick Chart")
p1
```

The below candle stick chart contains series of red and green colour candle stick with high, low, open and close stock prices. Different candle stick patterns indicate different entry and exit points of the shares. Once the users reviews and compares the charts they will be able to identify the patterns for upward and downward movement. Number of guidelines is available to interpret the patterns but one pattern will not fit for all the stocks as well stock markets.

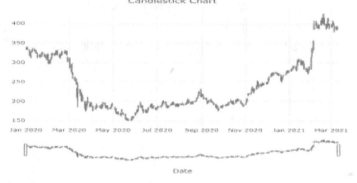

Relative Strength Index Chart

Relative Strength Index (RSI) helps us to identify the overbought state and oversold state which indicates the reversal of current trend. Normally above 70% RSI indicates overall bought state while below 30% indicate oversold state (These limits are suggestive and will not be always holds good. It depends on the market and individual stock).

```
Library(TTR)
di <- RSI(data1$Close.Price)
di1 <- RSI(data1$Close.Price, n=14,
maType="WMA", wts=data1$No.of.Shares)
df1<-data.frame(data1$Date,di1)
ggplot(df1,aes(data1.Date,di1))+geom_line(
color="blue")
```

We can use TTR package to compute the RSI index. After calculating the index we will create new data frame and use it for plotting the values. We will use number of shares as the weight here.

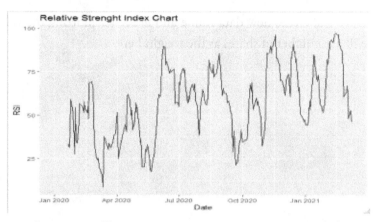

Stochastic Oscillator

Stochastic Oscillator Indicates overbought and oversold levels at 80% and 20%(These limits suggestive and will not be always holds good. It depends on the market and individual stock).

We will use TTR package and its function stoch to calculate the Stochastic Oscillator. We need to create data frame of high, low and close price of the stock as below

```
library(TTR)
hcldata<-
data.frame(data1$High.Price,data1$Low.Price,data
1$Close.Price)
soc<-stoch(hcldata, n.fastK=14)
soc1<-as.data.frame(soc)
soc1$idu<-as.numeric(row.names(soc1))
ggplot(soc1,aes(x=idu,y=fastK))+geom_line()
ggplot(soc1, aes(x=idu)) +
  geom_line(aes(y=fastK, color="fastK")) +
  geom_line(aes(y=fastD, color="fastD"))
```

Here will be creating a data frame and index variable for plotting the fastK(%K) and fastD(%D) variables. FastK and FastD are %K and %D indicators. When FastK crosses FastD then it is a buy signal and sell signal is opposite of that

```
soc1<-as.data.frame(soc)
soc1$idx<-as.numeric(row.names(soc1))
ggplot(soc1,aes(x=idx,y=fastK))+geom_line()
ggplot(soc1, aes(x=idx)) +
  geom_line(aes(y=fastK, color="fastK")) +
  geom_line(aes(y=fastD, color="fastD"))
```

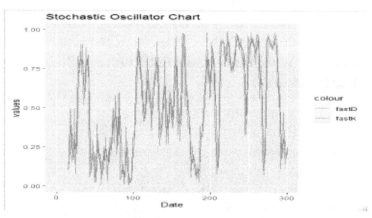

Average Directional Index

Average Directional Index measures the strength of the trend. We need to use close, high and low price to compute the index.

Strength of trend is strong if ADX is above 25 and strength of trend will be weak if ADX is below 20(These limits suggestive and will not be always holds good. It depends on the market and individual stock).

We need to use TTR package and its ADX function. Here the ADX value needs to be converted into data frame for plotting the ADX curve. We will be creating an index variable for the x axis.

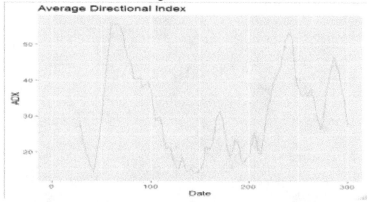

Bollinger Band

It is defined by three lines one is middle (simple moving average), upper and lower lines are +2 or -2 standards deviation from the moving average. When closing price is near the upper band then it indicates the stock is overbought and when it is near the lower band then it indicates the stock is oversold.

We need to use TTR package and its BBands function using High, Low and Close price data set. Here the BBands value needs to be converted into data frame for plotting the BBands curve. We will be creating an index variable for the x axis. Here three curves will be fitted - one is for upper, another is for lower and last one is for moving averages. The upper and lower band curves are 2 standard deviations from the moving averages curve.

```
bb1<-BBands(hcldata)
bb2<-as.data.frame(bb1)
bb2$idx<-as.numeric(row.names(bb2))
ggplot(bb2, aes(x=idx)) +
  geom_line(aes(y=dn, color="dn")) +
  geom_line(aes(y=mavg, color="mavg")) +
  geom_line(aes(y=up, color="up")) +
  labs(x="Date",y="values",title="Bollinger Bands")
```

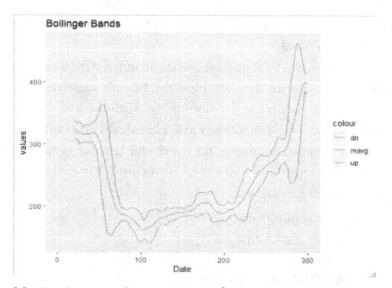

Moving Averages Convergence and Divergence

Moving Averages Convergence and Divergence (MACD) indicator shows the relationship between 12 day moving average and 26 day moving average. Along with MACD, a 9 day moving average line is plotted and if the MACD is above that line then it indicates a buy signal and if the MACD is below that line then it indicates a sell signal.

We need to use TTR package and its MACD function. We will be using close price, 12day (nFast), 26 day(nSlow) and 9 day (sSig) moving averages for the calculation of MACD. Here the MACD value needs to be converted into data frame for plotting the MACD curve.

We will be creating an index variable for the x axis. Here two curves will be fitted one is for MACD and another is for 9 day moving average which is denoted as signal curve.

```
macd1<-MACD(data1$Close.Price,nFast = 12,
nSlow = 26, nSig = 9)
macd2<-as.data.frame(macd1)
macd2$idx<-as.numeric(row.names(macd2))
ggplot(macd2, aes(x=idx)) +
 geom_line(aes(y=macd, color="macd")) +
 geom_line(aes(y=signal, color="signal")) +
 labs(x="Date",y="values",title="MACD")
```

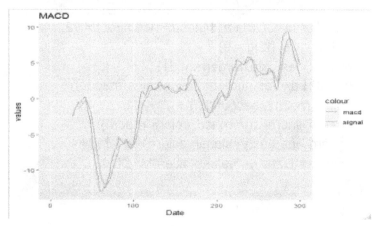

References

1. Chootong, C., & Sornil, O. (2012). Trading Signal Generation Using A Combination of Chart Patterns and Indicators. International Journal of Computer Science Issues (IJCSI), 9(6), 202.

2. Thammakesorn, S., & Sornil, O. (2019, April). Generating trading strategies based on candlestick chart pattern characteristics. In Journal of Physics: Conference Series (Vol. 1195, No. 1, p. 012008). IOP Publishing.

3. Bollinger, J. (1992). Using bollinger bands. Stocks & Commodities, 10(2), 47-51.

4. Wang, J., & Kim, J. (2018). Predicting stock price trend using MACD optimized by historical volatility. Mathematical Problems in Engineering, 2018.

5. Gurrib, I. (2018). Performance of the Average Directional Index as a market timing tool for the most actively traded USD based currency pairs. Banks and Bank Systems, 13(3), 58-70.

6. Beckers, S. (1983). Variances of security price returns based on high, low, and closing prices. Journal of Business, 97-112.

7. Beyaz, E., Tekiner, F., Zeng, X. J., & Keane, J. (2018, June).

Comparing technical and fundamental indicators in stock price forecasting. In 2018 IEEE 20th International Conference on High Performance Computing and Communications; IEEE 16th International Conference on Smart City; IEEE 4th International Conference on Data Science and Systems (HPCC/SmartCity/DSS) (pp. 1607-1613). IEEE.

8. Taran-Morosan, A. (2011). The relative strength index revisited. African Journal of Business Management, 5(14), 5855.

9. Wickham, H. (2011). ggplot2. Wiley Interdisciplinary Reviews: Computational Statistics, 3(2), 180-185.

10. Ulrich, J., Ulrich, M. J., & RUnit, S. (2020). Package 'TTR'.

11. Sievert, C. (2020). Interactive web-based data visualization with R, plotly, and shiny. CRC Press.

12. Ryan, J. A., Ulrich, J. M., Thielen, W., Teetor, P., Bronder, S., & Ulrich, M. J. M. (2020). Package 'quantmod'.

13. Dragulescu, A. A., Dragulescu, M. A. A., & Provide, R. (2020). Package 'xlsx'. Cell, 9(1).

14. Grolemund, M. G., & Wickham, H. (2013). Package 'lubridate'.

15. Mailund, T. (2019). Manipulating data frames: dplyr. In R Data Science Quick Reference (pp. 109-160). Apress, Berkeley, CA.

16. Svetunkov, I. (2017). Statistical models underlying functions of 'smooth'package for R.

17. Borchers, H. W., & Borchers, M. H. W. (2021). Package 'pracma'.

18. Hyndman, M. R. J., Akram, M., Bergmeir, C., O'Hara-Wild, M., & Hyndman, M. R. (2018). Package 'Mcomp'.

R software packages used

1. https://cran.r-project.org/package=ggplot2
2. https://cran.r-project.org/package=plotly
3. https://cran.r-project.org/package=TTR
4. https://cran.r-project.org/package=Mcomp
5. https://cran.r-project.org/package=pracma
6. https://cran.r-project.org/package=smooth
7. https://cran.r-project.org/package=quantmod
8. https://cran.r-project.org/package=dplyr
9. https://cran.r-project.org/package=lubridate
10. https://cran.r-project.org/package=xlsx

Chapter 4: Stock price prediction using Statistical tools

There are several Statistical tools such as Time series and regression analysis tools are used for predicting the stock price. Time series tools include simple moving averages, exponential moving averages and Autoregressive Integrated Moving Averages (ARIMA). Readers are encouraged to refer author's previous book on Business Intelligence: An Overview for basic statistical concepts (ISBN: 979-8724184502)

Time series is defined as series of observations related to a particular variable collected with respect to time. The time value can be days, month or year. In case of stock price, the time series includes price of stock recorded day wise.

Time series includes the following four components

   a. **Trend (T)** – It indicates the changes in the mean value of the stock over a period of time. It can be increasing or decreasing over a period of time.

   b. **Seasonal (S)** – It indicates the variation in the stock price within a year caused by factors such as weather or regular events such as festival

   c. **Cyclical (C)** – It is similar to seasonal component but time period will be usually more than a year(s). Cyclical components may repeat itself after a gap of years and runs for a particular period.

   d. **Irregular (I)** – It indicates the fluctuation in the stock price due to unknown factors which are not accounted by the above three components.

Additive and multiplicative models based on the above four
components are available to study the time series. Additive model
includes (T+S+C+I) and multiplicative model includes (T*C*S*I).

Decomposition function helps us to decompose the trend, seasonal
and irregular components of the time series using additive or
multiplicative model.

```
Library(xlsx)
Library(forecast)
Library(tseries)
data1<-read.xlsx('test2.xlsx',sheetIndex = 1)
tsdata<-data1 %>%
  group_by(year(Date), month(Date)) %>%
  summarize(Meanprice = mean(Close.Price,
na.rm = TRUE),
        Medianprice=median(Close.Price))
stprice <- ts(tsdata$Meanprice, frequency=12,
start=c(2015,1))
```

We
will use our extended sample data set which includes 5 years data and
can be downloaded from author's website. We need to transform the
data set into time series data set by aggregating the values by month and
covert into time series data.

```
stpricecom<-decompose(stprice)
plot(stpricecom,col="green",lwd=2)
```

Here stprice is the transformed time series data set with 12 data for each year starting from year 2015. We will use decompose function to decompose stprice data set and plot the same.

THE BELOW GIVEN CHART includes 4 curves the top one is actual monthly data, second is trend component, third is seasonal component and the last one is irregular component of the stock price time series. Here the time is given in years starting from 2015 to 2021.

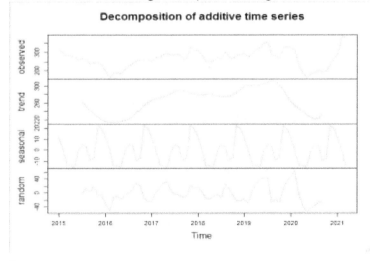

Lag

The term k^{th} lag is defined as the difference between the value and kth value in the time series.

Lag 1 is defined as the difference between the value and previous value.

Auto Correlation

Auto Correlation in a time series is defined as the measure of relationship between a particular value and k^{th} value in the same series. The following code provides auto correlation plot

```
acf(data1$Close.Price)
```

Partial Auto Correlation

```
acf(data1$Close.Price)
```

Partial Auto Correlation is similar to auto correlation except it considers only the item and k^{th} item ignoring the intermediate items effect.

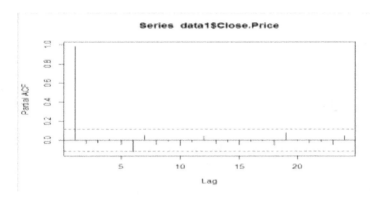

Series data1$Close.Price

STATIONARY

A time series is said to be stationary if the mean and variance of the series is constant over time.

Augmented Dickey Fuller Test

Augmented Dickey Fuller Test is used to test whether a time series is stationary or not. Here we will be having two hypotheses (statements)

1. Null Hypothesis : The series is non-stationary
2. Alternative Hypothesis : The series is stationary

If the probability value is less than the 0.05 we reject the null hypothesis and conclude that the series is stationary.

```
adf.test(data1$Close.Price)
```

```
Augmented Dickey-Fuller Test

data:  data1$Close.Price
Dickey-Fuller = -1.2943, Lag order = 6, p-value =
0.8737
alternative hypothesis: stationary
```

Here the p value is more than 0.05 hence the series is non-stationary.

We can make time series stationary by using methods like differencing which taking difference between the value and the previous value and continue this for all value thus making a new series with differenced values.

The following code provides differenced series and its stationary status

```
news1 <- diff(data1$Close.Price, differences=1)
adf.test(news1)
```

```
          Augmented Dickey-Fuller Test

data:  news1
Dickey-Fuller = -5.9862, Lag order = 6, p-value =
0.01
alternative hypothesis: stationary
```

As the p value is less than 0.05 we can conclude that the differenced time series is stationary.

Simple Moving Average (SMA)

Simple Moving Average (SMA) is used to smooth the noise or short term variations in the time series by averaging m values in the time series. Normally period m will be 5 and in case of stock price series it will be 5 day moving average or it can be 3 day moving average. Here the average is computed for every 3 or 5 days and then that smoothed series will be used instead of the original series in the future calculations such as forecasting.

We can use sma function and movavg function to calculate and compute the Simple Moving Average plot.

```
day5<-sma(data1$Close.Price,n=5)
plot(movavg(data1$Close.Price, 5, "s"), type = "l",
col = 1,main = "Simple Moving Averages", xlab =
"Days", ylab = "Share Price")
```

```
Time elapsed: 3.2 seconds
Model estimated: SMA(1)
Initial values were produced using backcasting.
Loss function type: MSE; Loss function value:
56.1116
Error standard deviation: 7.5159
Sample size: 300
Number of estimated parameters: 2
Number of degrees of freedom: 298
Information criteria:
   AIC    AICc    BIC    BICc
2063.566 2063.606 2070.973 2071.089
```

THE FOLLOWING OUTPUT and plot is obtained

Here Akaike Information Criterion (AIC) and Bayesian Information Criterion are used for selecting best model out of the different models built using the same data. The smaller the value of AIC the better is the model.

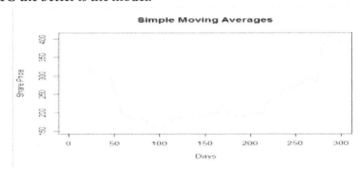

Exponential Moving Averages

Exponential Moving Averages are similar but assigns more weights to the recent observation than the older ones.

We can use EMA function and plot function to calculate and compute the Exponential Moving Average plot.

```
ema5<-EMA(data1$Close.Price,n=5)
plot(ema5, type = "l", col = "Green",main =
"Exponential Moving Averages", xlab = "Days",
ylab = "Share Price")
```

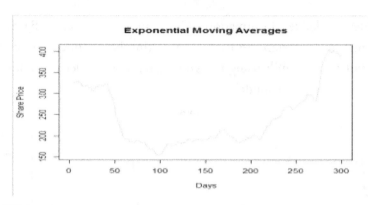

AUTO REGRESSIVE INTEGRATED Moving Averages (ARIMA)

Auto Regressive Integrated Moving Averages (ARIMA) model helps us to analyse the time series data and carry out forecasting functions on the data.

It helps us to identify the trend through the auto regressive method, make the series stationary through differencing and smooth the time series through moving averages.

It includes three parameters p,d and q to carry out the above functions.

1. p is the number of lags or preceding values to be used for time series. It will be normally 1 as we will be using the value and its preceding values in the regression part. (AR – Auto Regressive part)

2. d is the differencing the value used for making the time series stationary. If its value is 0 in the model then the series is already stationary (I - Integration part)

3. q is the moving average term and usually it will be 1 (MA – Moving Average part)

Based on the above parameters we can fit different models to see which model is the best one to fit by referring the AIC values of the models.

```
arima(data1$Close.Price,order=c(1,0,1))
arima(data1$Close.Price,order=c(1,1,1))
arima(data1$Close.Price,order=c(1,2,1))
arima(data1$Close.Price,order=c(1,2,2))
arima(data1$Close.Price,order=c(3,2,2))
```

The following code will helps us to build the ARIMA Models.

```
Coefficients:
         ar1    ma1  intercept
       0.9955 0.0482  307.7998
s.e.   0.0041 0.0551   66.4501
sigma^2 estimated as 55.98: log likelihood = -
1031.84, aic = 2071.68
```

```
Coefficients:
      ar1     ma1
    0.8980  -0.8416
s.e.  0.1152   0.1425
sigma^2 estimated as 55.36: log likelihood = -
1024.36,  aic = 2054.72
```

```
Coefficients:
      ar1     ma1
    0.0216  -0.9774
s.e.  0.0592   0.0133
sigma^2 estimated as 55.78: log likelihood = -
1023.56,  aic = 2053.13
```

```
Coefficients:
        ar1    ma1    ma2
      -0.7880 -0.1226 -0.8364
s.e.  0.1005  0.0820  0.0793
sigma^2 estimated as 55.13: log likelihood = -
1021.85, aic = 2051.7
```

```
Coefficients:
        ar1    ar2    ar3    ma1    ma2
      -0.7209 0.0535 0.1415 -0.2174 -0.7494
s.e.  0.1002 0.0735 0.0601  0.0853  0.0828
sigma^2 estimated as 54.05: log likelihood = -
1018.92, aic = 2049.84
```

AIC VALUE IS HIGHER in the first model and from second model onwards there is a slight reduction in the AIC values.

```
h<-auto.arima(data1$Close.Price)
```

We can also use auto.arima function to let the system choose the best model parameters.

WE CAN FIT THE DIFFERENT plots such as fitted values plot, residual plot from the ARIMA model parameters obtained from the ARIMA Model.

```
plot(h$fitted)
plot(h$x,col="red")
lines(h$fitted,col="blue")
plot(h$residuals)
```

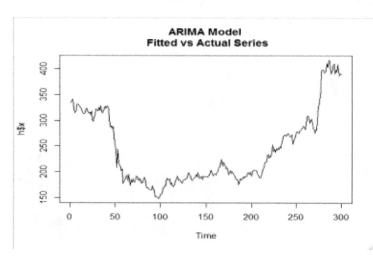

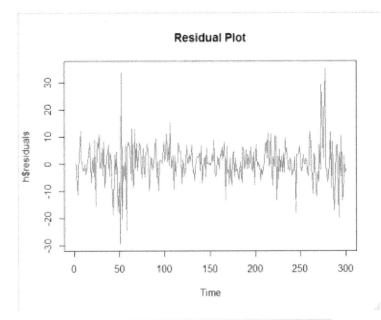

Residual Plot

```
AF = auto.arima(data1$Close.Price)
AFpred = forecast(AF, h = 10)
plot(AFpred, main = "Forecast using ARIMA")
```

WE CAN USE FORECAST function to forecast the future values using the fitted ARIMA Model.

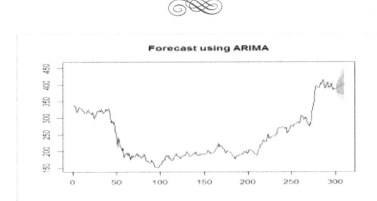

Forecast using ARIMA

REFERENCE

1. Wei, W. W. (2006). Time series analysis. In The Oxford Handbook of Quantitative Methods in Psychology: Vol. 2.
2. Hamilton, J. D. (2020). Time series analysis. Princeton university press.
3. Chatfield, C., & Xing, H. (2019). The analysis of time series: an introduction with R. CRC press.
4. Kirchgässner, G., Wolters, J., & Hassler, U. (2012). Introduction to modern time series analysis. Springer Science & Business Media.
5. West, M. (1997). Time series decomposition. Biometrika, 84(2), 489-494.
6. Theodosiou, M. (2011). Forecasting monthly and quarterly time series using STL decomposition. International Journal of Forecasting, 27(4), 1178-1195.
7. Adebiyi, A. A., Adewumi, A. O., & Ayo, C. K. (2014). Comparison of ARIMA and artificial neural networks models for stock price prediction. Journal of Applied Mathematics, 2014.
8. Jarrett, J. E., & Kyper, E. (2011). ARIMA modeling with intervention to forecast and analyze Chinese stock prices. International Journal of Engineering Business Management, 3(3), 53-58.
9. https://www.bseindia.com/
10. Holt, C. C. (2004). Forecasting seasonals and trends by exponentially weighted moving averages. International journal of forecasting, 20(1), 5-10.
11. Johnston, F. R., Boyland, J. E., Meadows, M., & Shale, E. (1999). Some properties of a simple moving average when applied to forecasting a time series. Journal of the Operational Research Society, 50(12), 1267-1271.

12. Ming-Ming, L., & Siok-Hwa, L. (2006). The profitability of the simple moving averages and trading range breakout in the Asian stock markets. Journal of Asian Economics, 17(1), 144-170.

13. Okpara, G. C. (2010). Stock market prices and the random walk hypothesis: Further evidence from Nigeria. Journal of Economics and International Finance, 2(4), 049-057.

14. Jagwani, J., Gupta, M., Sachdeva, H., & Singhal, A. (2018, June). Stock price forecasting using data from yahoo finance and analysing seasonal and nonseasonal trend. In 2018 Second International Conference on Intelligent Computing and Control Systems (ICICCS) (pp. 462-467). IEEE.

15. Chi, W. L. (2018, May). Stock price forecasting based on time series analysis. In AIP Conference Proceedings (Vol. 1967, No. 1, p. 040032). AIP Publishing LLC.

16. Mathew, O. O., Sola, A. F., Oladiran, B. H., & Amos, A. A. (2013). Prediction of stock price using autoregressive integrated moving average filter ((ARIMA (p, d, q))). Global Journal of Science Frontier Research, 13(8), 79-88.

17. Whittle, P. (1953). Estimation and information in stationary time series. Arkiv för matematik, 2(5), 423-434.

18. Grenander, U., & Rosenblatt, M. (2008). Statistical analysis of stationary time series (Vol. 320). American Mathematical Soc..

19. Hall, A. (1994). Testing for a unit root in time series with pretest data-based model selection. Journal of Business & Economic Statistics, 12(4), 461-470.

R software packages used

1. https://cran.r-project.org/package=forecast
2. https://cran.r-project.org/package=tseries

Chapter 8: Stock price prediction using Support Vector Machine (SVM)

Stock price predictions can be done using Machine Learning models where the system learns from the data set and apply the learned knowledge to the new data set for classification and prediction purposes.

There are two types of Machine Learning Algorithms are available one is supervised and another is unsupervised. Supervised algorithm divides the data set into training set and test data set. Training data set is used to train the model and test data set is used to test efficacy and accuracy of the model. The training data set contains the label which is to be predicted or classified whereas the test data set will not contain the label which needs to be predicted or classified.

Unsupervised algorithm does not use the training data set and uses the similarities or differences among the members of the data set to classify or identify patterns in the data set.

Support Vector Machine (SVM) is one of the supervised learning algorithm which is used for both classification and regression problems.

In classification problem Support Vector Machine is used to find the hyperplane and decision boundaries which classifies the data set into two classes. The same is applied to new data and the new data points will be classified into either of the two classes. The training data set is used to find the hyperplane and decision boundaries and test data set is used to test the model with new data set.

In regression problem, we will try to find the hyperplane and decision boundaries which best fit the data set. We can use the SVM algorithm to fit and evaluate the model for predicting the stock price by splitting the data set into training and test data set.

The stock prediction process can be done by both regression and classification problem.

The functions such as Room Mean Square Error (RMSE), Mean Square Error (MSE) and Mean Absolute Error (MAE) help us to evaluate the accuracy of the predicted model. Mean Square Error is nothing but the average squared deviation between the predicted and actual stock price.

```
library(e1071)
library(caret)
library(DescTools)
library(xlsx)
```

We will use the r packages such as e1071, caret and DescTools to build the SVM model for the stock price prediction

WE WILL SELECT ONLY the required columns and define as a new data set.

```
data1<-read.xlsx('test.xlsx',sheetIndex = 1)
datanew<-
data1[c('Close.Price','Open.Price','High.Price','Lo
w.Price','No.of.Shares','No..of.Trades')]
```

THE NEW DATA SET WILL be transformed using preprocess function of the caret package. The transformed data set will be split into train and test data set.

```
datam<-
preProcess(datanew,method=c('center','scale'))
datatrans<- predict(datam, datanew)
train <- datatrans[1:250,]
test <- datatrans[251:300,]
```

SVM MODEL IS BUILT by using closing price as response variable and all other variables such as open price, high, low, volume, number of quantity, number of trades as independent variables. We can add more variables like Moving Average values, volatility index to increase the prediction accuracy.

```
svmmodel<-svm(Close.Price~
Open.Price+High.Price+Low.Price+No.of.Shares
+No..of.Trades, data=train)
```

```
svm(formula  =  Close.Price  ~  Open.Price  +
High.Price + Low.Price + No.of.Shares +
   No..of.Trades, data = train)
Parameters:
SVM-Type:  eps-regression
 SVM-Kernel:  radial
     cost: 1
     gamma: 0.2
     epsilon:  0.1
Number of Support Vectors:  45
```

THE PREDICTED MODEL parameters are given below

The above model indicates it is a SVM regression model and uses radial basis function for its keral operation which is used to transform the data set.

We will use predict function of the caret package to predict the values of stock price using test data set. We can plot both predicted value of the stock price and actual values of the stock in the chart as below.

```
svmpred = predict(svmmodel, test)
x= 251:300
plot(x, test$Close.Price, pch=18, col="gray",ylim
= c(100,500))
lines(x, pred, col="green")
```

THE RMSE, MAE, MSE function of the caret package is used to calculate the following parameters to evaluate the model.

```
mse = MSE(test$Close.Price, svmpred)
mae = MAE(test$Close.Price, svmpred)
rmse = RMSE(test$Close.Price, svmpred)
```

```
> mse
[1] 2.138016
> mae
[1] 1.087352
> rmse
[1] 1.462196
```

REFERENCES

1. Leung, C. K. S., MacKinnon, R. K., & Wang, Y. (2014, July). A machine learning approach for stock price prediction. In Proceedings of the 18th International Database Engineering & Applications Symposium (pp. 274-277).

2. Patel, J., Shah, S., Thakkar, P., & Kotecha, K. (2015). Predicting stock and stock price index movement using trend deterministic data preparation and machine learning techniques. Expert systems with applications, 42(1), 259-268.

3. Shah, V. H. (2007). Machine learning techniques for stock prediction. Foundations of Machine Learning| Spring, 1(1), 6-12.

4. Vohra, A. A., & Tanna, P. J. (2021). A Survey of Machine Learning Techniques Used on Indian Stock Market. In IOP Conference Series: Materials Science and Engineering (Vol. 1042, No. 1, p. 012021). IOP Publishing.

5. Vijh, M., Chandola, D., Tikkiwal, V. A., & Kumar, A. (2020). Stock closing price prediction using machine learning techniques. Procedia Computer Science, 167, 599-606.

6. Munde, A., Jadhav, A., Kaute, H., & Gosavi, A. (2021). Automated Stock Trading Using Machine Learning. Available at SSRN 3772584.

7. Lin, Y., Guo, H., & Hu, J. (2013, August). An SVM-based approach for stock market trend prediction. In The 2013 international joint conference on neural networks (IJCNN) (pp. 1-7). IEEE.

8. Fenghua, W. E. N., Jihong, X. I. A. O., Zhifang, H. E., & Xu, G. O. N. G. (2014). Stock price prediction based on SSA and SVM. Procedia Computer Science, 31, 625-631.

9. Ince, H., & Trafalis, T. B. (2008). Short term forecasting with support vector machines and application to stock price

prediction. International Journal of General Systems, 37(6), 677-687.

10. Rustam, Z., & Kintandani, P. (2019). Application of Support Vector Regression in Indonesian Stock Price Prediction with Feature Selection Using Particle Swarm Optimisation. Modelling and Simulation in Engineering, 2019.

11. Karazmodeh, M., Nasiri, S., & Hashemi, S. M. (2013). Stock price forecasting using support vector machines and improved particle swarm optimization. Journal of Automation and Control Engineering, 1(2), 173-176.

12. Bao, Y., Lu, Y., & Zhang, J. (2004, September). Forecasting stock price by SVMs regression. In International conference on artificial intelligence: methodology, systems, and applications (pp. 295-303). Springer, Berlin, Heidelberg.

R software packages used

1. https://cran.r-project.org/package=e1071
2. https://cran.r-project.org/package=caret

Chapter 5: Stock price prediction using Artificial Neural Network (ANN)

Artificial Neural Network is one of the Supervised Machine Learning algorithm which works on the principle of human nervous system. It works well on the nonlinear data as most of the real world data sets will not follow the linear pattern and also can handle complex data sets.

Artificial Neural Network consists of input layer, hidden layers and output layer. Input layer receives the input data and hidden layer process the same by assigning weights and pass on to the next layer. Before the final output is produced by the output layer, during the training phase the system compares the output produced with actual output and uses back propagation method to adjust weights so that the error between the actual and predicted output is minimum.

We can use the neuralnet package to build the ANN stock price prediction model. We need to preprocess the data set before proceeding with the model building. Normalization can be done using different methods such as Min-Max, Range, Box-Cox transformation using the preprocess function of the caret package

As in the case of SVM model, we will split the data set into test and train data set. ANN model is built by using closing price as response variable and all other variables such as open price, high, low, volume, number of quantity, number of trades as independent variables. We can add more variables like Moving Average values, volatility index to increase the prediction accuracy.

We will use the following packages to build the ANN model

```
Library(neuralnet)
library(e1071)
library(caret)
library(DescTools)
library(xlsx)
```

WE WILL SELECT ONLY the required columns and define as a new data set. The new data set will be transformed using preprocess function of the caret package. The transformed data set will be split into train and test data set.

```
data1<-read.xlsx('test.xlsx',sheetIndex = 1)
datanew<-
data1[c('Close.Price','Open.Price','High.Price','Lo
w.Price','No.of.Shares','No..of.Trades')]
datam<-
preProcess(datanew,method=c('center','scale'))
datatrans<- predict(datam, datanew)
train <- datatrans[1:250,]
test <- datatrans[251:300,]
```

```
annmodel<-neuralnet(Close.Price~
Open.Price+High.Price+Low.Price+No.of.Shares
+No..of.Trades,
```

We will build the neural net model using the neuralnet package. Here will use the option such as number of hidden layers and linear output is true

```
$response
   Close.Price
1   1.309208599
2   1.380578165
3   1.300557743
4   1.087169951
5   1.077077285
$covariate
     Open.Price  High.Price  Low.Price
No.of.Shares No..of.Trades
1   1.3016430384 1.246339666 1.355108333 -
1.388098069 -1.159959297
2   1.3066862583 1.303265099 1.371869044 -
1.242546470 -1.055777119
3   1.3520752371 1.276937086 1.352922154 -
1.308825046 -1.020444016
4   1.2656200394 1.191548936 1.145963810 -
0.946762666 -0.257585499
5   1.1503464426 1.120392145 1.111713662 -
0.740965431 -0.179583468
$model.list
$model.list$response
[1] "Close.Price"
$model.list$variables
[1] "Open.Price"  "High.Price"  "Low.Price"
"No.of.Shares" "No..of.Trades"
```

THE FOLLOWING OUTPUT is produced.

The above model can be shown in the plot using plot function

```
plot(annmodel)
```

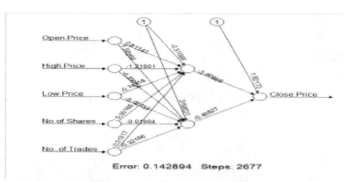

Error: 0.142894 Steps: 2677

```
annpred = predict(annmodel, test)
x= 251:300
plot(x,         test$Close.Price,         pch=18,
col="gray",main="Stock  Price  Predition  using
ANN", xlab="Days", ylab="Stock Price")
lines(x, annpred, col="green")
```

WE CAN PREDICT AND plot the model using the test data set.

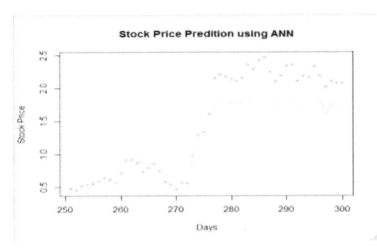

The RMSE, MAE, MSE function of the caret package is used to calculate the following parameters to evaluate the model.

```
mse = MSE(test$Close.Price, annpred)
mae = MAE(test$Close.Price, annpred)
rmse = RMSE(test$Close.Price, annpred)
```

```
> mse
[1] 0.08405745
> mae
[1] 0.2225649
> rmse
[1] 0.2899266
```

The following table provides comparative figures of MSE, MAE and RMSE of SVM and ANN Model in predicting using the test data set.

	MSE	MAE	RMSE
SVM	2.1380	1.0873	1.4621
ANN	0.08405	02225	0.2899

The above table shows the ANN model is performing better than SVM model.

References

1. Selvamuthu, D., Kumar, V., & Mishra, A. (2019). Indian stock market prediction using artificial neural networks on tick data. Financial Innovation, 5(1), 1-12.

2. Patel, M. B., & Yalamalle, S. R. (2014). Stock price prediction using artificial neural network. International Journal of Innovative Research in Science, Engineering and Technology, 3(6), 13755-13762.

3. Di Persio, L., & Honchar, O. (2016). Artificial neural networks architectures for stock price prediction: Comparisons and applications. International journal of circuits, systems and signal processing, 10(2016), 403-413.

4. Sureshkumar, K. K., & Elango, N. M. (2012). Performance analysis of stock price prediction using artificial neural network. Global journal of computer science and Technology.

5. Adebiyi, A. A., Ayo, C. K., Adebiyi, M. O., & Otokiti, S. O. (2012). Stock price prediction using neural network with hybridized market indicators. Journal of Emerging Trends in

Computing and Information Sciences, 3(1), 1-9.

6. Han, J. J., & Kim, H. J. (2021). Stock price prediction using multiple valuation methods based on artificial neural networks for KOSDAQ IPO companies. Investment Analysts Journal, 50(1), 17-31.

7. Gao, P., Zhang, R., & Yang, X. (2020). The application of stock index price prediction with neural network. Mathematical and Computational Applications, 25(3), 53.

R software packages used

1. https://cran.r-project.org/package=neuralnet
2. https://cran.r-project.org/package=e1071
3. https://cran.r-project.org/package=caret
4. https://cran.r-project.org/package=DescTools

Chapter 6: Stock price prediction using Decision Tree

Decision Tree is one of the Supervised Machine Learning Method where the decision such as classification or prediction is taken based on satisfaction of the condition. It includes a tree like a structure and starts with a root node. Here the node of the tree represents condition to be tested and internal node or branches indicate the possible outcomes from the test and leaf or terminal node represents the class label in the classification problem. This process is repeated till no more splitting is possible or increases in the classification accuracy.

Decision Tree works on the principle of greedy algorithm where in the data is split into subsets based on the satisfaction of the condition.

We will be using Decision Tree method as classification problem for our Stock price sample data set. We need to add a binary variable into the data set for the classification problem. We will store the increase or decrease status in the closing stock price when compared to the previous day closing price. If the closing price of the current day is increased from the previous day then status variable will have value 1 other wise 0.

The following code will add a new variable called hl by taking difference between the current value and previous value for the closing price variable.

```
datac <- within(data1, difference <-
c(NA,diff(Close.Price)))
datac1<-
```

WE WILL KEEP THE REQUIRED variable and split the data set into test and training data set using sampling function

```
set.seed(100)
datac2<-datac1[c(1:12,16)]
datapoints<-sample(1:300, size = 250 )
trainc<-datac2[datapoints,]
testc<-datac2[-datapoints,]
```

We can use rpart and rpart.plot function to build the decision model and decision tree plot. We can also calculate the accuracy of the decision tree model using predict and confusion matrix function.

```
library(rpart)
library(rpart.plot)
dtreefit <- rpart(as.factor(hl)~., data = trainc,
method = 'class')
rpart.plot(dtreefit)
predict1<-predict(dtreefit,testc[,-16],type="class")
confusionMatrix(predict1, as.factor(testc$hl))
```

Following is the summary of model obtained from the above code.

```
n=249 (1 observation deleted due to
missingness)
node), split, n, loss, yval, (yprob)
     * denotes terminal node
```

```
  2) X..Deli..Qty.to.Traded.Qty>=17.72 183  76 0
(0.5846995 0.4153005)
  4) Total.Turnover..Rs..< 1.150799e+09 155  52
0 (0.6645161 0.3354839)
    8) Spread.High.Low>=13.875 15  0 0
(1.0000000 0.0000000) *
    9) Spread.High.Low< 13.875 140  52 0
(0.6285714 0.3714286)
      18) No..of.Trades>=35821 8  0 0
(1.0000000 0.0000000) *
      19) No..of.Trades< 35821 132  52 0
(0.6060606 0.3939394)
        38) No.of.Shares< 3117175 90  28 0
(0.6888889 0.3111111)
          76) No..of.Trades>=15647 44  8 0
(0.8181818 0.1818182) *
          77) No..of.Trades< 15647 46  20 0
(0.5652174 0.4347826)
            154) No..of.Trades< 14389.5 37  13 0
(0.6486486 0.3513514)
            308)
X..Deli..Qty.to.Traded.Qty>=23.005 15  3 0
(0.8000000 0.2000000) *
              309) X..Deli..Qty.to.Traded.Qty< 23.005
22  10 0 (0.5454545 0.4545455)
                618) Total.Turnover..Rs..<
3.502549e+08 14  4 0 (0.7142857 0.2857143) *
                619)
Total.Turnover..Rs..>=3.502549e+08 8  2 1
(0.2500000 0.7500000) *
            155) No..of.Trades>=14389.5 9  2 1
(0.2222222 0.7777778) *
```

THE SAME MODEL IS GIVEN as plot

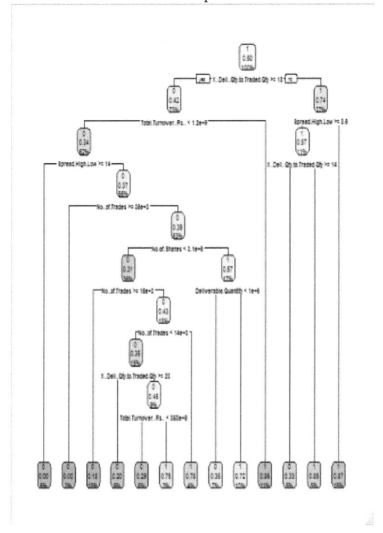

THE FOLLOWING GIVES the prediction and confusion matrix result

```
Confusion Matrix and Statistics
       Reference
Prediction  0  1
        0  9 13
        1 10 18
            Accuracy : 0.54
              95% CI : (0.3932, 0.6819)
 No Information Rate : 0.62
 P-Value [Acc > NIR] : 0.9040
               Kappa : 0.0527
 Mcnemar's Test P-Value : 0.6767
         Sensitivity : 0.4737
         Specificity : 0.5806
      Pos Pred Value : 0.4091
      Neg Pred Value : 0.6429
          Prevalence : 0.3800
      Detection Rate : 0.1800
 Detection Prevalence : 0.4400
    Balanced Accuracy : 0.5272
      'Positive' Class : 0
```

Here the model accuracy is 0.54 which may be due to the selection input variables in the model.

References

1. Wu, M. C., Lin, S. Y., & Lin, C. H. (2006). An effective application of decision tree to stock trading. Expert Systems with applications, 31(2), 270-274.
2. Tsai, C. F., & Wang, S. P. (2009, March). Stock price forecasting by hybrid machine learning techniques. In Proceedings of the international multiconference of engineers and computer scientists (Vol. 1, No. 755, p. 60).
3. Nair, B. B., Mohandas, V. P., & Sakthivel, N. R. (2010). A decision tree—rough set hybrid system for stock market trend prediction. International Journal of Computer Applications, 6(9), 1-6.
4. Kamble, R. A. (2017, June). Short and long term stock trend prediction using decision tree. In 2017 International Conference on Intelligent Computing and Control Systems (ICICCS) (pp. 1371-1375). IEEE.
5. Sorensen, E. H., Miller, K. L., & Ooi, C. K. (2000). The decision tree approach to stock selection. The Journal of Portfolio Management, 27(1), 42-52.
6. Li, W., & Liao, J. (2017, October). A comparative study on trend forecasting approach for stock price time series. In 2017 11th IEEE International Conference on Anti-counterfeiting, Security, and Identification (ASID) (pp. 74-78). IEEE.
7. Vaiz, S., & Ramaswami, M. (2016). A study on technical indicators in stock price movement prediction using decision tree algorithms. Am. J. Eng. Res, 5(12), 207-212.
8. Nugroho, F. S. D., Adji, T. B., & Fauziati, S. (2014, November). Decision support system for stock trading using multiple indicators decision tree. In 2014 The 1st

International Conference on Information Technology, Computer, and Electrical Engineering (pp. 291-296). IEEE.

R software packages used

1. https://cran.r-project.org/package=rpart
2. https://cran.r-project.org/package=rpart.plot

Chapter 7: Stock price prediction using Random Forest

R andom Forest is similar to Decision Tree algorithm which creates multiple trees from the subset of data which are selected at random from the main dataset. Each tree comes up with the classification of class or vote for that particular class. The final result is obtained by aggregating the votes from the different trees to arrive at the class label which is having more votes. It overcomes the over fitting problem of decision trees and also provides information about the variables which are important in classification task.

The data is divided into sub set of data through sampling with replacement technique and one third of the data (called out of bag data) is left for computing classification error.

We can use randomForest package for building the model. The following code will add a new variable called hl by taking difference between the current value and previous value for the closing price variable.

```
datac <- within(data1, difference <-
c(NA,diff(Close.Price)))
datac1<-
```

WE WILL KEEP THE REQUIRED variable and split the data set into test and training data set using sampling function

```
set.seed(100)
datac2<-datac1[c(1:12,16)]
datapoints<-sample(1:300, size = 250 )
trainc<-datac2[datapoints,]
testc<-datac2[-datapoints,]
```

We can use randomForest function to build the Random Forest model. We can also calculate the accuracy of the random forest model using predict and confusion matrix function.

```
RFfit <- randomForest(as.factor(hl)~., data =
trainc, importance=TRUE,

proximity=TRUE,na.action=na.exclude)
predict1<-predict(RFfit,testc[,-16],type="class")
confusionMatrix(predict1, as.factor(testc$hl))
```

```
RFfit
Call:
 randomForest(formula = as.factor(hl) ~ ., data =
trainc, importance = TRUE,      proximity = TRUE,
na.action = na.exclude)
               Type of random forest: classification
                     Number of trees: 500
No. of variables tried at each split: 3
        OOB estimate of  error rate: 36.95%
Confusion matrix:
   0  1 class.error
0 82 42  0.3387097
1 50 75  0.4000000
```

THE FOLLOWING MODEL summary and confusion matrix is obtained from the above code

```
Confusion Matrix and Statistics

        Reference
Prediction  0  1
       0  12 14
       1  7 17
           Accuracy : 0.58
             95% CI : (0.4321, 0.7181)
 No Information Rate : 0.62
 P-Value [Acc > NIR] : 0.7683
              Kappa : 0.168
 Mcnemar's Test P-Value : 0.1904
        Sensitivity : 0.6316
        Specificity : 0.5484
     Pos Pred Value : 0.4615
     Neg Pred Value : 0.7083
         Prevalence : 0.3800
     Detection Rate : 0.2400
Detection Prevalence : 0.5200
   Balanced Accuracy : 0.5900

      'Positive' Class : 0
```

Here the model accuracy is 0.58 which may be due to the selection input variables in the model.

References

1. Khaidem, L., Saha, S., & Dey, S. R. (2016). Predicting the direction of stock market prices using random forest. arXiv preprint arXiv:1605.00003.

2. Ballings, M., Van den Poel, D., Hespeels, N., & Gryp, R. (2015). Evaluating multiple classifiers for stock price direction prediction. Expert systems with Applications, 42(20), 7046-7056.

3. Kumar, M., & Thenmozhi, M. (2006, January). Forecasting stock index movement: A comparison of support vector machines and random forest. In Indian institute of capital markets 9th capital markets conference paper.

4. Patel, J., Shah, S., Thakkar, P., & Kotecha, K. (2015). Predicting stock and stock price index movement using trend deterministic data preparation and machine learning techniques. Expert systems with applications, 42(1), 259-268.

5. Ma, Y., Han, R., & Fu, X. (2019, October). Stock prediction based on random forest and LSTM neural network. In 2019 19th International Conference on Control, Automation and Systems (ICCAS) (pp. 126-130). IEEE.

6. Vijh, M., Chandola, D., Tikkiwal, V. A., & Kumar, A. (2020). Stock closing price prediction using machine learning techniques. Procedia Computer Science, 167, 599-606.

7. Park, J. S., Cho, H. S., Lee, J. S., Chung, K. I., Kim, J. M., & Kim, D. J. (2019, October). Forecasting Daily Stock Trends Using Random Forest Optimization. In 2019 International Conference on Information and Communication Technology Convergence (ICTC) (pp. 1152-1155). IEEE.

8. Kompella, S., & Chakravarthy Chilukuri, K. C. C. (2020).

Stock Market Prediction Using Machine Learning Methods. International Journal Of Computer Engineering And Technology, 10(3), 2019.

R software packages used

1. https://cran.r-project.org/package=randomForest

Chapter 8: Stock price prediction using Naïve Bayes method

N aïve Bayes algorithm is one of the supervised machine learning algorithm which uses Bayesian probability concept and treats the all the features (variables) of the data set are independent of each other.

We can use naïvebayes package to build the Naïve Bayes package.

The following code will add a new variable called hl by taking difference between the current value and previous value for the closing price variable.

```
datac <- within(data1, difference <-
c(NA,diff(Close.Price)))
datac1<-
```

WE WILL KEEP THE REQUIRED variable and split the data set into test and training data set using sampling function

```
set.seed(100)
datac2<-datac1[c(1:12,16)]
datapoints<-sample(1:300, size = 250 )
trainc<-datac2[datapoints,]
testc<-datac2[-datapoints,]
```

We can use navibayes function to build the Naïve Bayes model. We can also calculate the accuracy of the Naive Bayes model using predict and confusion matrix function.

```
library(naivebayes)
nbfit <-naive_bayes(as.factor(hl)~., data = trainc)
predict1<-predict(nbfit,testc[,-16],type="class")
confusionMatrix(predict1, as.factor(testc$hl))
```

```
========================================
=====Naive Bayes
========================================
=====
 Call:
naive_bayes.formula(formula = as.factor(hl) ~ .,
data = trainc)
Laplace smoothing: 0
A priori probabilities:

    0      1
0.497992 0.502008
 Tables:
::: Open.Price (Gaussian)
Open.Price     0       1
    mean 243.86855 242.82400
      sd  69.34896  69.31673
::: High.Price (Gaussian)
High.Price     0       1
    mean 245.80000 249.09000
      sd  69.64943  70.68310
::: Low.Price (Gaussian)
Low.Price      0       1
```

THE FOLLOWING MODEL summary and confusion matrix is obtained from the above code

```
    mean 236.51774 240.09720
     sd    67.97461  69.00138
::: Close.Price (Gaussian)
Close.Price       0        1
     mean 238.71613 246.46320
      sd   68.59839  69.75872
::: WAP (Gaussian)
    WAP          0        1
  mean 240.85040 244.93997
   sd    68.85258  69.76121
# ... and 7 more tables
```

```
              Reference
Prediction  0  1
         0 16 24
         1  3  7
              Accuracy : 0.46
                95% CI : (0.3181, 0.6068)
    No Information Rate : 0.62
    P-Value [Acc > NIR] : 0.9926460
                  Kappa : 0.0559
 Mcnemar's Test P-Value : 0.0001186
            Sensitivity : 0.8421
            Specificity : 0.2258
         Pos Pred Value : 0.4000
         Neg Pred Value : 0.7000
             Prevalence : 0.3800
         Detection Rate : 0.3200
   Detection Prevalence : 0.8000
       Balanced Accuracy : 0.5340
        'Positive' Class : 0
```

Here the model accuracy is 0.54 which may be due to the selection input variables in the model.

References

1. Patel, J., Shah, S., Thakkar, P., & Kotecha, K. (2015). Predicting stock and stock price index movement using trend deterministic data preparation and machine learning techniques. Expert systems with applications, 42(1), 259-268.
2. Milosevic, N. (2016). Equity forecast: Predicting long term stock price movement using machine learning. arXiv preprint arXiv:1603.00751.
3. Nair, B. B., Mohandas, V. P., & Sakthivel, N. R. (2010). A decision tree—rough set hybrid system for stock market trend prediction. International Journal of Computer Applications, 6(9), 1-6.
4. Udomsak, N. (2015). How do the naive Bayes classifier and the Support Vector Machine compare in their ability to forecast the Stock Exchange of Thailand?. arXiv preprint arXiv:1511.08987.
5. Chia-Cheng, C., Liu, Y., & Hsu, T. H. (2019). An analysis on investment performance of machine learning: an empirical examination on taiwan stock market. International Journal of Economics and Financial Issues, 9(4), 1.
6. Ballings, M., Van den Poel, D., Hespeels, N., & Gryp, R. (2015). Evaluating multiple classifiers for stock price direction prediction. Expert systems with Applications, 42(20), 7046-7056.

R software packages used

1. https://cran.r-project.org/package=naivebayes

Chapter 9: Stock price prediction using Deep Learning

D eep Learning models are extension of Machine Learning models which includes more number of hidden layers or hidden artificial neural network layers.

There are different packages are used to build the Deep Learning models which includes Keras, Tensorflow and H2O. We will be using H2O package for building the stock price prediction model using deep learning algorithm.

Using the following code we need to first initiate and import the CSV file into R studio environment. We will select only the required columns from the data set.

```
Library(h2o)
h2o.init()
datacsv<-h2o.importFile("test3.csv")
datacsv1<-datacsv[c(2,3,4,5,6,7,8)]
head(datacsv1)
```

WE NEED TO CREATE THREE sub data sets by splitting the main data set into train (60%), test(20%) and validation data sets (20%).

```
splits <- h2o.splitFrame(df, c(0.6,0.2),
seed=1234)
train  <- h2o.assign(splits[[1]], "train.hex")
valid  <- h2o.assign(splits[[2]], "valid.hex")
```

WE NEED TO DEFINE DEPENDENT and independent variables
for model prediction using set statement.

```
dependent <- "Close"
independent <- setdiff(names(train), y)
```

WE WILL BUILD THE MODEL using deeplearning function as
follows with hidden layers and ephocs and get the summary of the
model using summary statement.

```
Stockmodel <- h2o.deeplearning(
 x=independent,
 y=dependent,
 training_frame=train,
 validation_frame = vaild,
 hidden=c(12,11),
 epochs=0.2
 #balance_classes=T   ## enable this for high
class imbalance
)
summary(stockmodel)
```

```
H2ORegressionModel: deeplearning
Model Key:
DeepLearning_model_R_1617023050698_1
Status of Neuron Layers: predicting Close,
regression, gaussian distribution, Quadratic loss,
251 weights/biases, 7.8 KB, 19 training samples,
mini-batch size 1
```

The following summary is obtained

```
  layer units    type dropout    l1    l2
mean_rate rate_rms momentum mean_weight
1   1  12   Input 0.00 %    NA    NA
NA     NA     NA       NA
2   2   10 Rectifier  0.00 % 0.000000 0.000000
0.001865 0.001823 0.000000   0.004858
3   3   10 Rectifier  0.00 % 0.000000 0.000000
0.004550 0.011023 0.000000   -0.001082
4   4   1   Linear    NA 0.000000 0.000000
0.000337 0.000179 0.000000   0.092347
  weight_rms mean_bias bias_rms
1    NA     NA     NA
2  0.288951  0.499709 0.005917
3  0.305295  0.999562 0.003974
4  0.510780  0.001695 0.000000
H2ORegressionMetrics: deeplearning
** Reported on training data. **
** Metrics reported on full training frame **
MSE: 3057.905
RMSE: 55.29832
MAE: 40.48649
RMSLE: 0.2024574
Mean Residual Deviance : 3057.905
** Metrics reported on full validation frame **
MSE: 3178.988
RMSE: 56.38252
MAE: 40.44809
RMSLE: 0.1995131
Mean Residual Deviance : 3178.988
```

```
Variable Importances:
  variable relative_importance scaled_importance
percentage
1   High         1.000000          1.000000
0.217337
2  Trades        0.971689          0.971689
0.211183
3   Open         0.813119          0.813119
0.176720
4   WAP          0.731922          0.731922
```

THE MODEL SUMMARY ABOVE provides the both training and validation data set MSE, RMSE (on the original scale of the data set) and along with importance of each independent variable in predicting the closing price of the stock.

Now we can use predict function to predict the model with the test data set. We can also plot the actual and predicted values by creating a data frame from the predicted and actual values.

```
stockpred <- h2o.predict(stockmodel, test)
ht<-as.data.frame(test$Close)
hm<-as.data.frame(stockpred$predict)
x1=1:62
htm<-data.frame(x1,ht,hm)
ggplot(htm, aes(x=x1, y=predict)) +
geom_point(col="red") +
geom_line(aes(x=x1,y=Close)) +
labs(x="Days",y="Stock value",title="Stock price
predicting using Deep Learning")
```

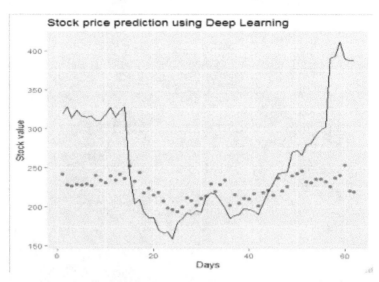

The difference between the predicted and actual value may be due to the choice of independent variables.

References

1. Khare, K., Darekar, O., Gupta, P., & Attar, V. Z. (2017, May). Short term stock price prediction using deep learning. In 2017 2nd IEEE international conference on recent trends in electronics, information & communication technology (RTEICT) (pp. 482-486). IEEE.

2. Hossain, M. A., Karim, R., Thulasiram, R., Bruce, N. D., & Wang, Y. (2018, November). Hybrid deep learning model for stock price prediction. In 2018 IEEE Symposium Series on Computational Intelligence (SSCI) (pp. 1837-1844). IEEE.

3. Nikou, M., Mansourfar, G., & Bagherzadeh, J. (2019). Stock price prediction using DEEP learning algorithm and its comparison with machine learning algorithms. Intelligent Systems in Accounting, Finance and Management, 26(4), 164-174.

4. Sen, J., & Datta Chaudhuri, T. (2018, December). Stock price prediction using machine learning and deep learning

frameworks. In Proceedings of the 6th International Conference on Business Analytics and Intelligence, Bangalore, India.

5. Mehtab, S., & Sen, J. (2020). A time series analysis-based stock price prediction using machine learning and deep learning models. arXiv preprint arXiv:2004.11697.

6. Yu, P., & Yan, X. (2020). Stock price prediction based on deep neural networks. Neural Computing and Applications, 32(6), 1609-1628.

7. Singh, R., & Srivastava, S. (2017). Stock prediction using deep learning. Multimedia Tools and Applications, 76(18), 18569-18584.

8. Cho, C. H., Lee, G. Y., Tsai, Y. L., & Lan, K. C. (2019, December). Toward stock price prediction using deep learning. In Proceedings of the 12th IEEE/ACM International Conference on Utility and Cloud Computing Companion (pp. 133-135).

9. Jain, S., Gupta, R., & Moghe, A. A. (2018, December). Stock price prediction on daily stock data using deep neural networks. In 2018 International Conference on Advanced Computation and Telecommunication (ICACAT) (pp. 1-13). IEEE.

10. Nabipour, M., Nayyeri, P., Jabani, H., Mosavi, A., & Salwana, E. (2020). Deep learning for stock market prediction. Entropy, 22(8), 840.

11. https://cran.r-project.org/package=h2o

12. https://docs.h2o.ai/h2o-tutorials/latest-stable/tutorials/ deeplearning/index.html

Chapter 10: Stock price prediction using Recurrent Neural Network (RNN)

Recurrent Neural Networks work on the principles of Artificial Neural Network but uses the output of the previous layer as input of the next layer. It adopts the same parameters for processing throughout the network. It is suitable for sequence data such as text processing and stock price predictions.

We can use keras package to build the classification model using RNN model. Here we will build classification model instead of regression model. To build a classification model we need to create a class variable called hl which includes values 1 and 0. If the value of the current day closing price is greater than previous days close price then it contains value 1 otherwise 0. We will select required variable and omit the NA values. As the first contains no difference value it will be represented by NA hence we need to drop the first row from the data set for our analysis purpose.

```
Library(xlsx)
Library(keras)
data1<-read.xlsx('test.xlsx',sheetIndex = 1)
datac <- within(data1, difference <-
c(NA,diff(Close.Price)))
datac1<-
transform(datac,hl=ifelse(difference>0,1,0))
set.seed(100)
datac2<-datac1[c(1:12,15)]
data2<-na.omit(datac2)
data2<-data2[-1]
```

We will create two separate data frames one is for independent variable or features and other is for response or dependent variable from the main data set. We will also create an index which will be used to split the data set into training and test data set

```
X<-data2[,1:11]
y<-data2[,12]
partindex <- createDataPartition(y, p = .9,
                      list = FALSE,
                      times = 1)
```

We will create two training data sets which include independent variables set and another is dependent variable or response variable.

Here the original dimension of the data set is only two dimensions one is for rows and another is for variable. RNN or Keras sequential model requires three dimensional data sets the extra one is used for sequencing which is nothing but the time stamp. So we need to reshape the data set using matrix and array function.

```
X_train <- as.matrix(X[partindex,])
X_train1<-array(X_train, dim =
c(length(partindex), 11, 1))
y_train <- y[partindex]
dim(X_train1)
```

```
dim(X_train1)
[1] 270  11   1
```

THE SAME NEEDS TO BE done for the test data set also.

```
X_test <- as.matrix(X[-partindex,])
X_test1<-array(X_test, dim = c( length(y)-
length(partindex), 11, 1))
y_test <- y[-partindex]
```

WE WILL NOW BUILD THE RNN model using keras_model_sequential function. The model includes two dense layer and one RNN layer with 11 units which corresponds to the feature vectors or independent variables. The model summary is given below.

```
model <- keras_model_sequential()
model %>%
  layer_dense(input_shape = dim(X_train1)[2:3],
units = 11)
model %>%
  layer_simple_rnn(units = 11)
model %>%
  layer_dense(units = 1, activation = 'sigmoid') #
summary(model)
```

```
Model: "sequential_3"
Layer (type)                    Output Shape
Param #
dense_6 (Dense)                 (None, 11, 11)
22
simple_rnn_3 (SimpleRNN)            (None,
11)                 253
dense_7 (Dense)                 (None, 1)
12
Total params: 287
Trainable params: 287
Non-trainable params: 0
```

We will compile and fit the model using compile and fit function
of keras package.

```
model %>% compile(loss = 'binary_crossentropy',
            optimizer = 'RMSprop',
            metrics = c('accuracy'))

model <- model %>% fit(
  x = X_train1,
  y = y_train,
 batch_size = 32,
  epochs = 20,
  validation_split = 0.1)

model
```

The following summary is obtained

```
Trained on 243 samples (batch_size=32,
epochs=20)
Final epoch (plot to see history):
    loss: 0.6829
  accuracy: 0.572
  val_loss: 0.7204
val accuracy: 0.4074
```

The same can be represented as plot as given below. The plots provide information about loss, validation loss. It also provides accuracy and loss with respect to training data and validation datasets.

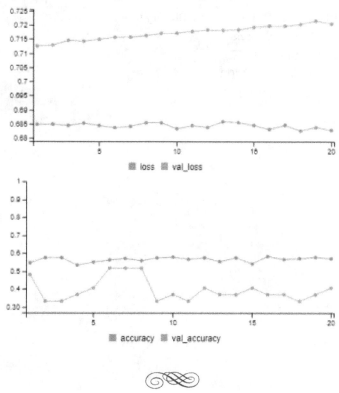

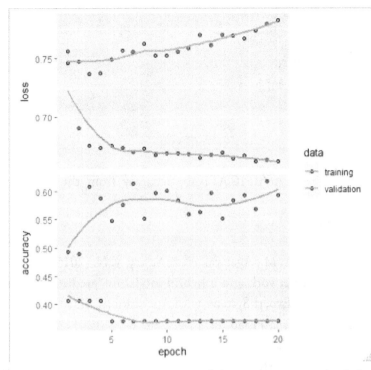

THE MODEL PROVIDED 57% and 40.7% training and validation accuracy. The above obtained accuracy is may be due to choice of input variables for the model

We can also create confusion matrix to know the difference between predicted and actual values

```
classes <- model %>% predict_classes(X_test1,
batch_size = batch_size)
table(y_test, classes)
```

THE FOLLOWING SUMMARY is obtained.

```
classes
y_test  0  1
    0   10 3
    1    7 9
```

HERE THE CLASSIFICATION accuracy from the test data is 65.2% (19/29)

References

1. Rather, A. M., Agarwal, A., & Sastry, V. N. (2015). Recurrent neural network and a hybrid model for prediction of stock returns. Expert Systems with Applications, 42(6), 3234-3241.
2. Hsieh, T. J., Hsiao, H. F., & Yeh, W. C. (2011). Forecasting stock markets using wavelet transforms and recurrent neural networks: An integrated system based on artificial bee colony algorithm. Applied soft computing, 11(2), 2510-2525.
3. Samarawickrama, A. J. P., & Fernando, T. G. I. (2017, December). A recurrent neural network approach in predicting daily stock prices an application to the Sri Lankan stock market. In 2017 IEEE International Conference on Industrial and Information Systems (ICIIS) (pp. 1-6). IEEE.
4. Gao, Q. (2016). Stock market forecasting using recurrent neural network (Doctoral dissertation, University of Missouri—Columbia).
5. Gao, T., & Chai, Y. (2018). Improving stock closing price prediction using recurrent neural network and technical indicators. Neural computation, 30(10), 2833-2854.
6. Gupta, S. Deep Learning: Big Tech Stock Predictions Using Recurrent Neural Networks (RNN).
7. Zhao, J., Zeng, D., Liang, S., Kang, H., & Liu, Q. (2020).

Prediction model for stock price trend based on recurrent neural network. Journal of Ambient Intelligence and Humanized Computing, 1-9.

8. Qiu, Y., Yang, H. Y., Lu, S., & Chen, W. (2020). A novel hybrid model based on recurrent neural networks for stock market timing. Soft Computing, 1-18.

9. Berradi, Z., Lazaar, M., Omara, H., & Mahboub, O. (2020). Effect of Architecture in Recurrent Neural Network Applied on the Prediction of Stock Price. IAENG International Journal of Computer Science, 47(3).

10. Rikukawa, S., Mori, H., & Harada, T. (2020). Recurrent neural network based stock price prediction using multiple stock brands. International Journal of Innovative Computing, Information and Control, 16(3), 1093-1099.

11. Васяева, Т. А., Мартыненко, Т. В., Хмелевой, С. В., & Андриевская, Н. К. (2020). Stock Prices Dynamics Forecasting with Recurrent Neural Networks. Открытые семантические технологии проектирования интеллектуальных систем, (4), 277-282.

12. Taylor, O. E., Ezekiel, P. S., & Deedam-Okuchaba, F. B. Stock Price Prediction Using Recurrent Neural Network Architecture.

13. Nabipour, M., Nayyeri, P., Jabani, H., Mosavi, A., & Salwana, E. (2020). Deep learning for stock market prediction. Entropy, 22(8), 840.

14. Gao, P., Zhang, R., & Yang, X. (2020). The application of stock index price prediction with neural network. Mathematical and Computational Applications, 25(3), 53.

Chapter 11: Stock price prediction using Long Short Term Memory (LSTM)

$\mathbf{S}$ tock price prediction using Long Short Term Memory model is similar to Recurrent Neural Network. Recurrent Neural Networks work on the principles of Artificial Neural Network but uses the output of the previous layer as input of the next layer. It can hold the information in the memory only in the short term and hence it is affected by the vanishing gradient problem.

LSTM overcomes the vanishing gradient problem of Recurrent Neural Network by using its gates to store the information for a long period of time and controls the flow of information. The gates decide which information to keep or which information to discard. The property of keeping information long term will be helpful in solving problems like text processing and stock price prediction problems.

We can use keras package as done in the RNN model to build the classification model using LSTM algorithm. Here we will build classification model instead of regression model.

To build a classification model we need to create a class variable called hl which includes values 1 and 0. If the value of the current day closing price is greater than previous days close price then it contains value 1 otherwise 0.

We will select required variable and omit the NA values. As the first contains no difference value it will be represented by NA hence we need to drop the first row from the data set for our analysis purpose.

```
Library(xlsx)
Library(keras)
data1<-read.xlsx('test.xlsx',sheetIndex = 1)
datac <- within(data1, difference <-
c(NA,diff(Close.Price)))
datac1<-
transform(datac,hl=ifelse(difference>0,1,0))
set.seed(100)
datac2<-datac1[c(1:12,15)]
data2<-na.omit(datac2)
data2<-data2[-1]
```

We will create two separate data frames one is for independent variable or features and other is for response or dependent variable from the main data set. We will also create an index which will be used to split the data set into training and test data set

```
X<-data2[,1:11]
y<-data2[,12]
partindex <- createDataPartition(y, p = .9,
                    list = FALSE,
                    times = 1)
```

We will create two training data sets which include independent variables set and another is dependent variable or response variable.

Here the original dimension of the data set is only two dimensions one is for rows and another is for variable. RNN or Keras sequential model requires three dimensional data sets the extra one is used for sequencing which is nothing but the time stamp. So we need to reshape the data set using matrix and array function.

```
X_train <- as.matrix(X[partindex,])
X_train1<-array(X_train, dim =
c(length(partindex), 11, 1))
y_train <- y[partindex]
dim(X_train1)
```

```
dim(X_train1)
[1] 270  11   1
```

THE SAME NEEDS TO BE done for the test data set also.

```
X_test <- as.matrix(X[-partindex,])
X_test1<-array(X_test, dim = c( length(y)-
length(partindex), 11, 1))
y_test <- y[-partindex]
```

WE WILL NOW BUILD THE LSTM model using keras_model_sequential function. The model includes two dense layer and one LSTM layer with 11 units which corresponds to the feature vectors or independent variables. The model summary is given below.

```
model %>%
  layer_dense(input_shape = dim(X_train1)[2:3],
units = 11)%>%
  layer_lstm(units=11)%>%
  layer_dense(units = 1, activation = 'sigmoid')
  summary(model)
```

```
summary(model)
Model: "sequential_21"
Layer (type)                    Output Shape
Param #
dense_47 (Dense)                (None, 11, 11)
22
lstm_15 (LSTM)                  (None, 11)
1012
dense_46 (Dense)                (None, 1)
12
Total params: 1,046
Trainable params: 1,046
Non-trainable params: 0
```

We will compile and fit the model using compile and fit function of keras package.

```
model %>% compile(loss = 'binary_crossentropy',
           optimizer = 'sgd',
           metrics = c('accuracy'))

model3 <- model %>% fit(
 x = X_train1,
 y = y_train,
 batch_size = 32,
 epochs = 50,
 validation_split = 0.1)
```

The following summary is obtained

```
Trained on 243 samples (batch_size=32,
epochs=50)
Final epoch (plot to see history):
    loss: 0.6827
  accuracy: 0.5844
  val_loss: 0.7272
val_accuracy: 0.4444
```

The same can be represented as plot as given below. The plots provide information about loss, validation loss. It also provides accuracy and loss with respect to training data and validation datasets.

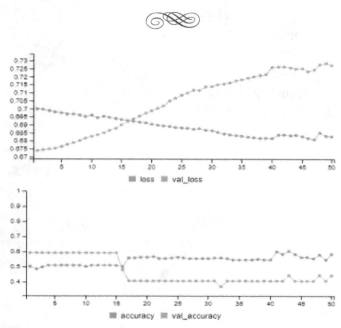

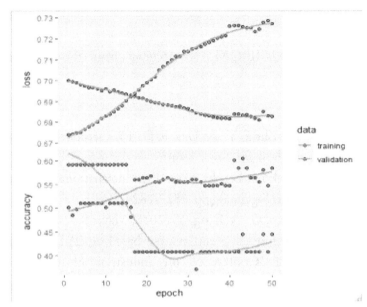

THE MODEL PROVIDED 58% and 44% training and validation accuracy. The above obtained accuracy is may be due to choice of input variables for the model

We can also create confusion matrix to know the difference between predicted and actual values

```
classes <- model %>% predict_classes(X_test1,
batch_size = batch_size)
table(y_test, classes)
```

THE FOLLOWING SUMMARY is obtained.

```
classes
y_test  0   1
     0  3  10
     1  2  14
```

HERE THE CLASSIFICATION accuracy from the test data is 58.6% (19/29)

References

1. Chen, K., Zhou, Y., & Dai, F. (2015, October). A LSTM-based method for stock returns prediction: A case study of China stock market. In 2015 IEEE international conference on big data (big data) (pp. 2823-2824). IEEE.
2. Liu, S., Liao, G., & Ding, Y. (2018, May). Stock transaction prediction modeling and analysis based on LSTM. In 2018 13th IEEE Conference on Industrial Electronics and Applications (ICIEA) (pp. 2787-2790). IEEE.
3. Nelson, D. M., Pereira, A. C., & de Oliveira, R. A. (2017, May). Stock market's price movement prediction with LSTM neural networks. In 2017 International joint conference on neural networks (IJCNN) (pp. 1419-1426). IEEE.
4. Roondiwala, M., Patel, H., & Varma, S. (2017). Predicting stock prices using LSTM. International Journal of Science and Research (IJSR), 6(4), 1754-1756.
5. Ding, G., & Qin, L. (2020). Study on the prediction of stock price based on the associated network model of LSTM. International Journal of Machine Learning and Cybernetics, 11(6), 1307-1317.
6. Ding, G., & Qin, L. (2020). Study on the prediction of stock price based on the associated network model of LSTM. International Journal of Machine Learning and Cybernetics, 11(6), 1307-1317.
7. Yan, Y. (2021, March). Prediction of Stock Price Based on LSTM Model. In 6th International Conference on Financial Innovation and Economic Development (ICFIED 2021) (pp. 199-206). Atlantis Press.

8. Ko, C. R., & Chang, H. T. (2021). LSTM-based sentiment analysis for stock price forecast. PeerJ Computer Science, 7, e408.

9. Hasan, M. M., Roy, P., Sarkar, S., & Khan, M. M. (2021, January). Stock Market PredictionWeb Service Using Deep Learning by LSTM. In 2021 IEEE 11th Annual Computing and Communication Workshop and Conference (CCWC) (pp. 0180-0183). IEEE.

R software packages used

1. https://cran.r-project.org/package=keras

Chapter 12: Stock price prediction using Text Mining models and Sentiment analysis

Apart from numeric data analysis, currently methods such as Text Mining, Natural Language Processing and Sentiment analysis techniques help us to analyze the data in textual form. The data in textual form includes social media content, blogs, news websites, stock trading sites which includes news about the stock, user's comments and opinion about the company, its financial status, stock price movement. This information also exhibits user's sentiment about the stock price whether the stock is performing well or not or it will increase or decrease in the future.

R packages such as tm, NLP, rvest, SentimentAnalysis are available to carry out the text based analysis. Before starting the text mining process one need to get the text data related to stock prices from sources like financial information sites, webpages and social media sites.

Social media sites like twitter provides Application Programming Interface (APIs) to download the tweets about the particular stock price. We can use web scrapping methods to extract the user's comments and opinion about the stock price from the stock trading websites. We can also download stock related news from sites like Yahoo finance and google finance sites through r packages function.

Once the text source is brought into R environment the other steps in the text mining and sentiment analysis remains same. We will be using hypothetical user's comments as data source and store it xlsx file. It includes date wise comments for the particular stock.

We will define packages using library statement

```
library(xlsx)
library(dplyr)
library(tm)
library(wordcloud2)
```

WE WILL IMPORT THE file into r environment and convert each comment as a file and combine the files into corpus using corpus function of tm package. We need to use UFT-8 character set to remove the special characters in the comments.

```
data1<-read.xlsx('stockcomment.xlsx',sheetIndex
= 1)
data1$COMMENT
corpus1 <- iconv(data1$COMMENT, to = "UTF-
8")
```

THE FOLLOWING DOCUMENT corpus is obtained.

```
<<SimpleCorpus>>
Metadata:  corpus specific: 1, document level
(indexed): 0
```

WE NEED TO PREPROCESS the document before moving to the analysis stage. We will have to remove blank spaces, punctuations, covert upper case letters to lower case letters, numbers, stop words like 'a', 'the', 'this' from the documents using tm_map function of the tm package. We can also remove specific words using tm map function option.

```
docs1 <- tm_map(docs,removeNumbers)
docs2 <- tm_map(docs1,removePunctuation)
docs3 <- tm_map(docs2,stripWhitespace)
docs4 <- tm_map(docs3,
content_transformer(tolower))
docs5 <- tm_map(docs4, removeWords,
stopwords("english"))
docs6 <- tm_map(docs5, removeWords, c("will"))
```

After cleaning the data, we need create Term document matrix and make it is as a matrix. The matrix obtained shows a particular term is present in a document or not. If the term is present it is represented as 1 otherwise 0 in the document

```
stockdtm <- TermDocumentMatrix(docs6)
stockmatrix <- as.matrix(stockdtm)
```

THE FOLLOWING MATRIX is obtained

```
Docs
Terms          1 2 3 4 5 6 7 8 9 10 11 12 13 14 15
16 17 18 19 20 21 22 23 24 25 26 27 28 29
  market       1 1 0 0 0 0 0 0 0 0 0 0 0 0 0
0 0 0 0 0 0 0 0 0 0 0 0 0
  soon         1 0 0 0 0 0 0 0 0 0 0 0 0 0 0
0 0 0 0 0 0 0 0 0 0 0 0 1
  stock        1 1 2 1 0 0 1 0 0 0 1 1 1 0 1 0 1
0 2 1 1 1 0 0 0 1 0 1 0
```

We calculate the word frequency using rowsums option of the data.frame function and we an plot wordcloud which is a graphical representation of words used by the users in the comments. The words which are used more often other than the usual stop words will be given more font weight and looks predominant in the word cloud. We will use wordcloud2 package to create the word cloud.

```
stockcloud <- data.frame(rownames(matrix),
rowSums(matrix))
wordcloud2(stockcloud,
        size = 0.7,
        minSize = 1)
```

We can carry out sentiment analysis to find the hidden sentiments in the comments given by the users. We will use packages such as SentimentAnalysis and syuzhet package.

Syuzhet package express sentiments in 8 categories such as Joy, Fear, Anticipation, Anger, sadness, surprise, Trust and disgust. We use get_nrc_sentiment function to obtain the sentiment which includes the english language dictionary to find the sentiments

```
library(syuzhet)
stocksent<-get_nrc_sentiment(corpus1)
head(stocksent)
```

THE FOLLOWING MATRIX is obtained which includes document and whether the document contains the sentiments or not.

	anger	anticipation	disgust	fear	joy	sadness	surprise	trust	negative	positive
1	0	0	0	0	0	0	0	0	0	0
2	1	0	0	0	0	0	0	0	1	0
3	0	2	0	0	0	0	0	0	0	0
4	1	0	0	0	0	0	0	1	1	1
5	0	2	0	1	0	0	0	1	1	1
6	0	2	0	0	2	1	0	3		

    We can plot the above sentiment scores as plot using the following code

```
barplot(colSums(stocksent[,
1:8]),col=coul,cex.names=.55,
    main="Sentiment Analysis",
    xlab="Sentiment Category",
    ylab="Sentiment Score")
```

The following bar chart on sentiment analysis with respect to 8 sentiment categories is obtained

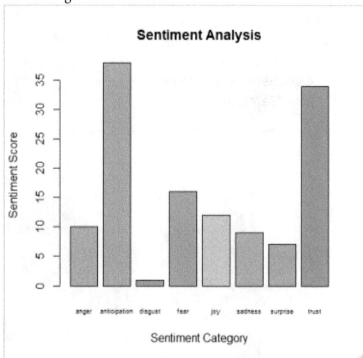

From the above chart we can say that the users expressed anticipation about the stock price movement and trust in the stock along with fear also.

References

1. Mittermayer, M. A. (2004, January). Forecasting intraday stock price trends with text mining techniques. In 37th Annual Hawaii International Conference on System Sciences, 2004. Proceedings of the (pp. 10-pp). IEEE.
2. Kalyani, J., Bharathi, P., & Jyothi, P. (2016). Stock trend prediction using news sentiment analysis. arXiv preprint arXiv:1607.01958.
3. Dickinson, B., & Hu, W. (2015). Sentiment analysis of

investor opinions on twitter. Social Networking, 4(03), 62.
4. Jaggi, M., Mandal, P., Narang, S., Naseem, U., & Khushi, M. (2021). Text Mining of Stocktwits Data for Predicting Stock Prices. Applied System Innovation, 4(1), 13.
5. De Fortuny, E. J., De Smedt, T., Martens, D., & Daelemans, W. (2014). Evaluating and understanding text-based stock price prediction models. Information Processing & Management, 50(2), 426-441.
6. Nikfarjam, A., Emadzadeh, E., & Muthaiyah, S. (2010, February). Text mining approaches for stock market prediction. In 2010 The 2nd international conference on computer and automation engineering (ICCAE) (Vol. 4, pp. 256-260). IEEE.
7. Cheng, S. H. (2010, July). Forecasting the change of intraday stock price by using text mining news of stock. In 2010 International Conference on Machine Learning and Cybernetics (Vol. 5, pp. 2605-2609). IEEE.
8. Huang, J. Y., & Liu, J. H. (2020). Using social media mining technology to improve stock price forecast accuracy. Journal of Forecasting, 39(1), 104-116.
9. Feuerriegel, S., & Gordon, J. (2018). Long-term stock index forecasting based on text mining of regulatory disclosures. Decision Support Systems, 112, 88-97.

Don't miss out!

Visit the website below and you can sign up to receive emails whenever Vinaitheerthan Renganathan publishes a new book. There's no charge and no obligation.

https://books2read.com/r/B-A-YASK-TELOB

BOOKS 2 READ

Connecting independent readers to independent writers.

Also by Vinaitheerthan Renganathan

Business Intelligence : an Overview
Stock Price Analysis Through Statistical And Data Science Tools: an Overview
Machine Learning Algorithms for Data Scientists: An Overview
Biostatistics Explored Through R Software: An Overview

Watch for more at www.vinaitheerthan.com.

www.ingramcontent.com/pod-product-compliance
Lightning Source LLC
Chambersburg PA
CBHW071206050326
40689CB00011B/2256